COMPETITION FRIENDLY PROTECTIONISM

How a Certain Kind of Protectionism Could Temper and Improve Globalisation.

Ronald Stuart

Grosvenor House
Publishing Limited

All rights reserved
Copyright © Robert Julian, 2012

Robert Julian is hereby identified as author of this
work in accordance with Section 77 of the Copyright, Designs
and Patents Act 1988

The book cover picture is copyright to Robert Julian

This book is published by
Grosvenor House Publishing Ltd
28-30 High Street, Guildford, Surrey, GU1 3EL.
www.grosvenorhousepublishing.co.uk

This book is sold subject to the conditions that it shall not, by way of
trade or otherwise, be lent, resold, hired out or otherwise circulated
without the author's or publisher's prior consent in any form of
binding or cover other than that in which it is published and
without a similar condition including this condition being imposed
on the subsequent purchaser.

A CIP record for this book
is available from the British Library

ISBN 978-1-903596-73-4

CONTENTS

PART ONE
Unintended Consequences

Chapter I Positive Externalities — 9

- What are Positive Externalities? or Capitalism as a System of Unintended Consequences
- Which Came First, the Chicken or the Egg?
- Five Forms of Positive Externalities
- Further Evidence for the Existence of Positive Externalities
- Which Economic Activities Produce Positive Externalities?

Chapter II Economic Activities Matter — 48

- The Logic of Industrial Policy
- Comparative Advantage versus Industrial Policy
- The Creation of Maximum Opportunity Instead of Maximum Capital
- The Different Needs and Character of the Pioneer versus the Emulator

CONTENTS

PART TWO
Business is War

Chapter III The Conflict of Trade Interests   68

- The Prize: Export-Led Growth in the Right Sectors
- The Arithmetic Problem: The Ultimate Check on Development
- The Conflict of Industrial Policy Players versus the Docile Harmony of Free Traders
- Game Theory and the Role of the WTO

Chapter IV The Winners and the Losers   87

- Five Examples of Winning
- Instances of Domination and Capitulation: From Hard Power Through to Ideology
- The Losers: Specialising in Being Poor
- The Limitations of Fair Trade Schemes

CONTENTS

PART THREE
Where are We Heading?

Chapter V   **The Developing Countries**   137

Chapter VI   **The Poor Countries**   141

– A Lesson from History on Relative Scarcity
– The Myth of Opportunity for All: Failure Built into the System
– Welcome to the State of Limbo: Stuck in the Reservoir

Chapter VII   **The Rich Countries**   160

– The End of Dominance
– Three Trends Shaping Our Future
– The Present Role of Technology and Innovation in Reconciling These Trends
– The Uncertainty of Relying on New Technology and Innovation

CONTENTS

PART FOUR
Tempering Globalisation

Chapter VIII   **Why Change is Inevitable**   196

- The Unsustainable Course we're Stuck On
- A Weakened Ideology
- Avoiding the Pitfalls of Protectionism

Chapter IX   **Competition-Friendly Protectionism**   215

- The Axis: Positive Externalities Once More, and an Explanation of Required Scope
- The Sectors Best Left to Their Own Devices
- The Prize Sector: Wake Up and Smell the Coffee, Name the Game and Share out the Spoils
- The Relocalisation Sector: The Least Worst Way to Achieve Progressive Goals
- Creating Intermediate Scope Markets: Reattempting Regional Trade Agreements Between Poor Countries
- Summary: Differentiation not Ideology
- Practical Issues to Consider

Bibliography   256

Introduction

This book is primarily about the nature of globalisation and trade and its dynamic effects on different countries' fortunes. It is not a technical study of the constituent parts of trade, but a discussion about its broad trends and long-term outcomes. It instead focuses on positive externalities and the inherent conflict of interests believed to be central to an anti-free market interpretation of trade relations. Its main conclusion is the controversial proposition that competition-friendly protectionism could be beneficial and viable in certain circumstances.

Economists such as Erik Reinert, Ha-Joon Chang and others have already established an effective and coherent critique of the present free market globalisation ideology. Therefore, although parts of those critiques are central to the point of view being put forward here, I have covered these unoriginal concepts as briefly as possible, while using citations heavily. It is possible that the amounts of extracted text maybe too great, but extracts are always the highlight of any book that I read and I hope they encourage wider reading here. Instead of repeating my version of established arguments, more space has been dedicated to what I hope are my more original, if less tested, thoughts and ideas. Although parts of this book may seem to follow the popular anti-free market narratives, do not expect a straightforward hymn in praise of these progressive views and industrial policy. In parts issue is also taken with some commonly held anti-free market assertions.

The style of analysis and argument within this book reflects a particular view that economics is more of a contestable subject

– and less a hard science – than many economists would perceive. As a result of this ethos, the task of this book cannot be to prove its thesis unequivocally, but to paint a revealing and convincing picture of the subject, which stands up on balance to different challenges to its thesis from history, rationality and common sense. I believe there is what Beinhocker calls an "availability bias" in economics and its practising professionals:

> "Availability Biases. People tend to make decisions based on data that is easily available as opposed to finding the data that is really needed to make a good decision. This is, in effect, 'looking for your lost keys under the lamppost' because that is where the light is best" (Beinhocker p. 122).

I would further add to this that for the most important economic issues and questions, much of the data "really needed" is not present or is impossible to collect. You cannot *prove* certain economic answers to me by hitting me with reams of numbers, so try to *convince* me instead. Therefore, there is less reliance on numerical evidence compared to what may be expected and often points made are deliberately less than absolute or conclusive.

> "In my view, it is best to consider all knowledge as tentative. The best scholars maintain an open-mindedness and humility about even their own core beliefs. Excessive conviction is often the sign of insufficient thought, which in turn may be derived from certain pigheadedness" (Greg Mankiw, web page).

It has been necessary in this book to generalise countries into three broad groups – rich countries, poor countries and developing countries – in order to distil the subject down into a manageable complexity. Given that a central theme within this book is that some undeveloped countries are actually not developing, the clumsy label of poor country has been resorted to as a label for this third group. It is hoped that the main themes, taken as a whole, will counterbalance and dissipate any slight offence caused in using this clumsy label and very rough suggested grouping of countries. Of course countries in all the groupings have very diverse and individual situations and histories, but it is hoped that it will be appreciated that generalisations are necessary in such a large subject.

As the many citations throughout should reflect, the excellent books of other favourite economists have been a main source of inspiration and information for parts of this book. However, this book remains a single-handed effort and as such, could be viewed very much as work in progress. Therefore, any wise advice, useful suggestions or constructive criticism will be gratefully and graciously received and may influence an improved, re-edited edition.

ronaldstuart@virginmedia.com

PART ONE

Unintended Consequences[1]

---
[1] "As always, capitalism must essentially be understood as a system of unintended consequences ..." (Reinert, p. 85)

Chapter I

Positive Externalities

"If we are fortunate, we will see US economic growth of about 3 percent per year in real terms over the next decades. Of this growth, about one-quarter—0.75 percent per year, say—will come from the labor side: more hands with more skills and more education. Another one-quarter will come from the capital side: plant and equipment purchases funded by investors. ... However, fully half of economic growth—1.5 percent per year—comes from technical and organisational progress: innovation. Economic growth arising from innovation is not captured by those who first undertake the innovations, create the technologies, or pioneer the organisations. These important fruits of innovation do not remain confined to the innovators but instead spill out in a capillary fashion into the broader economy, first to those nearby and later to those further away—if there is a later. Ford did not capture the lion's share of the gains from the Ford-invented and Ford-pioneered assembly line—General Motors, Caterpillar, Westinghouse, and many others shared them. Xerox did not capture any of the gains from the invention of the windows-icons-mouse-pointer computer interface—Apple and Microsoft did. Fully half of economic growth is an unrecompensed by-product of what businesses do. It spills out into the local industrial ecosystem." (Cohen & DeLong, p. 8-9).

What are Positive Externalities? or Capitalism as a System of Unintended Consequences

Positive externalities can be described as benefits from an economic activity that are received by people or organisations other than those who initiated the activity. They are also known in modern academia as spillovers, agglomerations or "capability-building" (Chang p. 215). However, "positive externalities" is a much broader, more technically specific economic term, and is therefore more appropriate for use here. For example, if I pay to have the road to my house upgraded from a mud and stone track to a tarmac road, my neighbours may benefit without having paid towards the project. These benefits are called externalities because they are *external* to the decision-maker's direct costs and benefits, and therefore external to the direct incentives which the initiator of the project experiences. So the benefit my neighbour receives is, in a financial sense, external to my decision of whether or not to improve my road.

The meaning of the positive part of the phrase 'positive externality' is obvious, although it is the opposite term of 'negative externality' that is traditionally studied more widely in economics. Capitalist economic systems are based on the premise that individuals and organisations can capture and are liable for the costs and benefits involved in and accruing from their actions and enterprises. The outcomes from these entrepreneurial actions in free market theory then combine to lead to the optimum use of resources within any environment, and ultimately should leave a profit for the business that has successfully undertaken the useful activity within the community. The study of externalities in traditional economics textbooks usually appears in the form of concerns that a particular market is not optimising in its outcomes, due to these external factors not being included in the incentives businesses face. Therefore, externalities being present in a market are a point of concern, due to the possibility that inefficient decisions (in an economy-wide sense, rather than an individual business sense) are being made.

Economics students will have learned how externalities can be used to consider the effectiveness or failure of specific markets to produce outcomes that reflect the true costs and benefits of actions and enterprises. For example, it would be a concern if the pollution that a business produces is not reflected in its products' prices or operational decisions. The field of mainstream economics does not, however, typically frame positive externalities as a primary source of economic progress and development, as this book claims. The positive externalities on which we focus are not centred on issues of market failure, but are concerned with all the many positive changes and factors which can emanate from the presence of particular economic activities in countries or localities. Thus, we are looking at the changes and factors that these business activities produce for others or for the future, that are not directly part of their business model. Therefore, businesses themselves usually do not initially benefit in their yearly profit and loss accounts from these unintended by-products. The scope of positive externalities can be very wide, diverse and even unpredictable, which, as we shall see, is part of their inherent quality for generating positive change.

As certain kinds of positive externalities are central to this book, it is important to identify these different types of externalities more clearly. However, this is a hard task, because inherent in the nature of externalities is that they are the most hidden and intangible factors present in business environments. They are inherently hard to assign a precise value to as they are rarely listed, bought or sold. For example, if I improve the road to my house, I probably do it based only on the costs and benefits a new road has to me. I would not attempt to quantify the exact monetary value the new road has to my neighbours. Furthermore, even if I consulted with my neighbour, she may see an opportunity to influence my altruistic considerations and inflate the value she claims the new road has to her. Or alternatively, if she perceives that I am going to go ahead anyway, she may deflate the value she claims it has to her, in order to deflate any financial or moral obligation she may foresee herself feeling towards me.

People and organisations in most other economic situations give tradable goods and economic factors a definite monetary value in a market backed by real behaviour. In other words, in most cases, this necessity to 'put their money where their mouth is' cuts through any ulterior motives to inflate or deflate without consequence, the values of their economic exchanges. In contrast, positive externalities by nature are not exposed to this real test of value, but reliant on subjective interpretation within complex and changing environments, and furthermore, when a value is sought, it may be interpreted by someone with an interest in inflating or deflating it.

Which Came First, the Chicken or the Egg?

> "As always, cumulative causations are behind both development and underdevelopment, creating 'virtuous' and 'vicious' circles." (Reinert, p. 181).

Before we look at the different kinds of positive externalities more closely in the next section, it is worth noting that a common theme in the character of positive externalities is their potential for being both a cause and an effect of successful economic activity. They can be assumed as being both a prerequisite for development and a product of development. This presents a problem typical to many areas of interpretation in economics: a situation in which two phenomena can be seen to rise or fall together in sequence, but different schools of thought or different observers tend to interpret the cause and effect relationship in two opposite ways. A further interpretation could identify or introduce a third common factor, which is then shown to be the real reason behind the apparently misunderstood relationship between the first two factors. Importantly, unlike more definite and absolute sciences such as physics, it often is the case that neither side is able to prove absolutely that its interpretation is correct beyond doubt.[2] This circular and contestable nature of the subject therefore makes positive externalities hard to study objectively, and more importantly, it could be argued, has historically obscured their true worth and recognition in mainstream economics. Although it is relatively easy to identify that these positive externality factors are present in an economic environment that already is developing strongly, it is and always has been open to debate whether they were there first and contributed to positive change, or whether they are a positive result of the change.

There could be several explanations as to why it could be alleged that positive externalities have been under-recognised by modern economics. One reason could be that economists prefer empirical proof and quantifiable data to pepper and solidify their assertions in order for them to gain professional merit, and areas where such proof and data are forthcoming are the areas upon which economists tend to build their careers. This is Bienhocker's "availability bias" as mentioned in the introduction. Economists would not want their contribution to economics or their 'life's work' to amount to a

---

[2] As a simple example for readers without a background in economics, consider three viewpoints based on observing the same country's economy. Viewpoint one—high wage deals from unions are causing high inflation. Viewpoint two—high inflation is causing a rising cost of living, which is causing higher pay deals. Viewpoint three—the government is printing too much money, which is causing high inflation *and* high pay deals together.

collection of vague, descriptive and subjective observations, which may be all that studies of positive externalities could ever generate. Economists are fond of considering the rational decisions actors make to maximise reward for their efforts, and perhaps this theory can also be applied to explain their own professional behaviour.

"...research in standard textbook economics, limited by its tools and assumptions, moves along the path of least mathematical resistance rather than one of maximum relevance" ... "the toolbox and the incentive system of the profession combine to make most economists prefer to be accurately wrong than approximately correct" ... "Physics-based models are also unable to handle novelty and innovations: that something qualitatively new can happen in the world. They also miss the synergies, linkages and systemic effects that constitute the glue that bonds economies and societies together" ... [they] "exclude precisely those factors that create wealth ... imperfect competition, innovations, synergies between economic sectors, economies of scale and scope and the presence of economic activities which make these factors possible" (Reinert, pp. 4 & 35 & 28 & 30).

"In the United States they are hardly discussed. American economists acknowledge externalities and even admit they can be important. But they are difficult to quantify and therefore suspect. If you want to be shunned as a retrograde mercantilist in a Washington economic policy discussion, one sure tactic is to suggest consideration of externalities" (Prestowitz, p. 209).

When considering all of the forms of positive externalities detailed below, it is possible to assert that a business would desire or require greater levels and volumes of these forms of positive externalities to be present before starting an enterprise. The successful business would also usually generate more of these positive externalities when it was successfully producing and performing. While accepting that all cases are different, if we can conclude generally that both cause and effect aspects are partially true in nearly all cases, this circular nature must also inherently be an acceleration factor within economic development, and therefore one cause of the momentum that seems to characterise a successful developing area or country.

Five Forms of Positive Externalities

Thus far, it has been proposed that a main source of economic development and prosperity are factors that are almost never fully identified, nearly impossible to value or measure, and neglected by economists as professionally unrewarding. Furthermore, when positive externalities are indeed recognised as co-existing with instances of development and prosperity, it is debatable which way the causation runs. Given these points, convincing the reader would seem a big ask. Below are the said positive externalities, which I have grouped into five general types.

a) Infrastructure

Infrastructure is perhaps one of the most overused words in development economics, but it is an important subject nonetheless. Traditionally, certain types of infrastructure are studied by economics students as a primary example of a special type of common, merit or public good, which should be given special consideration regarding state support or state regulation when organising and managing a market economy. The themes in the common good analysis parallel the themes in the positive externality subject discussed here. The shared theme is the inefficiency of the free market to provide the optimum level of certain goods, where the benefits or costs of producing the good are external to the individuals or organisations that are initiating the activity.

The dimension of positive externalities has implications for nearly all types of infrastructure, including services such as transport links, power supply, communication, legal business environment, law and order, national defence, and the development of a region's basic ability to construct, maintain and repair buildings and plants, and maintain all of the above. In nearly all of these areas, there are benefits to be had by companies that are not paid for, or only partly paid for, and therefore inherently also benefits given which are not and cannot be charged for, which are, of course, the positive externalities in question. I will not look at specific areas of infrastructure mentioned individually in detail, as each area is self-explanatory and it is clear what essentials businesses need to survive. Although many types of infrastructure have to be paid for directly by the business relative to consumption, and therefore in nature they are not all purely an externality, there is in all types of infrastructure a high fixed or investment that needs to be present prior to consumption. The cost per unit, or marginal cost, is then lower the more the infrastructure is used, as the high fixed cost is spread over a greater number of customers. Therefore, unless there are issues of limited resources (like a congestion or pollution issue, which would be a negative externality), the presence of one business using an infrastructure factor inherently benefits subsequent businesses, which is a positive externality given from the first enterprise to the second, and also often from the second enterprise to the first.

To explain this in the language of a non-economist, let's compare a company (local or foreign) wishing to start a business in a poor or developing country to a family going on a camping holiday. Running a business in a rich, developed country is comparable to living in a modern family home:

everything is available in the kitchens, bathrooms and bedrooms with which to provide efficiently and smoothly for the family's daily needs. The camper, on the other hand, is trying to exist in a more limited environment, and will not have many of these necessities and conveniences immediately present, like electricity, water, and all the other paraphernalia of modern living. The person at home in the modern house throughout the rest of the year can easily cope with most unexpected scenarios that happen, whereas with the camper, an illness, poor weather or the breakage or loss of some key piece of equipment can cause them to waste hours of time and effort resolving the issue. When you're camping, just providing and fulfilling the basic requirements of everyday living can take up half of the day (although that's part of the fun!) At home, however, the person usually has a full-time job, family commitments and other leisure activities to attend, and they take care of these basic everyday chores of living quickly and efficiently in between.

Examples of these infrastructure-related positive externalities could be found by considering the case of camping on a camp site, which results in other campers sharing the cost of the resources needed. The comparison could be made that the difference between starting a business in an area with or without other businesses present is like the difference between camping on a camp site with hundreds of customers throughout the year and building your own camp site in a field for you to use for just one week each year. On the widely used campsite, the campground owner has provided shower and toilet facilities, water and electricity supply, a small shop, rubbish collection, general maintenance and security. These services would be impractical and extremely expensive for one camper to provide for himself, but a campsite owner can provide them as a business and reclaim the large fixed initial expense from charging a small fee to a large number of campers.

As argued, the positive externalities contained within effective infrastructure are important in making an environment conducive to business. Successful examples of economic development show a balanced growth between the comprehensiveness of the infrastructure available to businesses and the advancing needs of the businesses in the region due to their growing sophistication. Growing one without the other is inefficient in one case, because no one is using the service, which may increase costs, and usually impossible in the other as the businesses fail. For example, a small farm growing traditional crops needs little infrastructure, an enterprise processing or packing and transporting food produce needs a little more, a T-shirt factory needs more again, and a car production factory needs very good infrastructure in its region. These crude examples show that the needs of businesses are different and need to be matched by a level of infrastructure within their environment. The history of attempts at new business and aid projects in poor countries is littered with instances where projects have failed due to the lack of infrastructure and technological capability. It is often proven that low-tech solutions are more appropriate in these environments, as machines have broken down or the complicated requirements for the long-term success of projects have not been fulfilled after the initial input of the project initiators.

b) Knowledge and Skills

> "Other countries look on these plants and centres not just as production units or even jobs, but also as universities and critical pathways to a better future. For them, a semiconductor plant doesn't just make chips: it gives several thousand people skills that are transferable to many other things. The plant establishes ties with suppliers who may in turn locate facilities near it and educate more people in the skills necessary to produce their products and services. It can be used as an R&D centre to develop new

products or even whole industries. It provides jobs that justify and encourage the teaching and study of technical disciplines. These so-called externalities, which are not a direct part of the production process, are actually more valuable to these countries than the production itself." (Prestowitz, p. 209).

Knowledge and skills are another well-trodden area of development economics, but it is useful to consider the area through the framework or lens of positive externalities given by organisations to subsequent organisations.

"It tends to be assumed that technological change and new innovations descend like manna from heaven, available free of charge to all ('perfect information'). It is not taken into consideration that knowledge—especially when it is new—has high costs and is not generally available. The knowledge is protected by huge barriers to entry, where economies of scale and accumulated experience are important elements in creating the barrier." (Reinert, p. 139).

Knowledge is considered here as information that can be written down and transmitted through education, formal training or formalised rules and procedures. But perhaps skills are more interesting because often they can only be *picked up* on the job, and not formally taught. It is easy to relate aspects of all jobs and professions that become either a motor skill like using a computer, or an intuitive skill in understanding what action is required for a specific situation, in a decision-making or management context. These positive externalities of knowledge and skills include all aspects of improving the industry-specific and transferable skills and knowledge of an area's population, which enriches the area's ability to succeed in future enterprises. Education is the most obvious provider of this kind of positive externality, which explains its high esteem among development economists and charity organisations. But also, positive externalities can develop from both formal knowledge transfer through the activities of a multinational company, or the informal natural development of learning by doing, connected with engaging in some new economic activity.

Even the most basic level of economic activity and production, people can often, in performing a job or task for a period of time, develop skills through 'learning by doing' and experimentation. It is this type of experience that planning committees of able professionals with no practical experience would never be able to develop. When given an opportunity, most people prove to be industrious, entrepreneurial and masters of their own working environment. People are quick to make use of opportunities for gaining from positive externalities in the form of learning from one another or other established businesses. Many professional jobs require years of training, knowledge and intelligence, but what is more significant – yet less generally appreciated – is how much experimentation, evolution and aptitude are developed by people in more modest roles in less-esteemed workplace activities. When considering one's own working life, it is easy to relate to the idea that 'learning by doing' is considerably more valuable than memorising processes and facts when improving someone's potential. Inherently and logically, a basic rule could be that doing an activity within an enterprise can provide a greater positive externality than not doing the activity.

This new knowledge, when shared and disseminated, is one of the most powerful positive externalities possible. It is a benefit for which the originator can never charge and which never shows up in any financial accounts, as it is external—a 'positive externality.' New businesses are often started by individuals who have left a larger company with both the knowledge of this section and the contacts of the next section. Skilled individuals can be spread out and used to train and disseminate best practices within companies during times of expansion. Likewise, a substantial fraction of corporate management expertise can be poached – but companies can still recover by constantly training and exposing themselves to experiences and new talent.

c) Networks and Contacts

Running all but the most basic business involves setting up numerous contacts and relationships in order to bring together all of the segments of a successful business, from factors of production to sale and profit. This process has the effect of creating many positive externalities, in that these contacts, relationships, networks and institutions can be then taken advantage of by future enterprises comprising of the same or different people. Most importantly, their use of these contacts and networks does not impinge upon any other business's ability to draw on the same resources. A large proportion of all manufactured goods consist of intermediate goods, which are not ready for sale to the final end consumer, but which are sold between firms. This point underlines the importance of networks, relationships and locations, as studied in the modern topic of cluster theories and economic geography. Particularly in an area such as contemporary international trade in manufactured goods, no one business can fulfil all of the functions necessary from raw material to point of sale, so contacts and relationships are exceedingly important. The old-fashioned trade fair, where producers gathered to drum up business and exchange ideas on technology, innovation and trends, is a very clear and bold example of a positive externality-boosting activity.

Networks and contacts can also become a coping strategy for those in a business or legal environment that is hostile or inadequate in its support of business and trade. In poor countries, the weak or corrupt enforcement of contracts, property rights and credit agreements can produce a business environment that is far less conducive to trade than the comprehensively regulated, developed country environment that is often taken for granted. Informal but strong networks, creating their own norms of behaviour and reputation-based incentives, can serve to replicate the sanctions of the missing effective infrastructure, and allow businesses to subsequently flourish in otherwise hostile environments. The classic case of the trade and business network creating its own relationships and norms in sub-optimum environments is the ethnic minority business network. The original and most famous examples were the Jews of Europe and the Mediterranean, but present examples include the Chinese in China's neighbouring countries, the Indians in East Africa, and the Lebanese in other parts of Africa. These all are examples of very effective ethnic-based networks, where the members create their own norms and use reputation and personal relationships to engender trust in hostile environments.

> "These ethnic networks solve many of the cheating problems. As one observer of the 'bamboo network' noted, if a Chinese businessman reneges on an agreement, he goes on the blacklist." (Easterly, p. 73).

The value of any established network route, contract relationship and working institution is an important positive externality that an area or organisation has to offer a new business. This acts as a free gift from the established business community to the new starter. It is all very well for the perfect competition theory ideology to assume that goods will be provided if there is a theoretical profit to be made, but without established contacts and trusted networks, most complex enterprises would not thrive.

d) Creativity and Diversity

Creativity and diversity are two additional types of positive externalities that particularly embody the above-mentioned issue of cause and effect. Creativity can describe the propensity of a region to generate or 'search out' new enterprises and new products which are original and fit for competition. Diversity is similar, describing not the originality but the mix of an area's economic activity. A diverse area or country would not have its eggs in one basket, or would have its finger in a lot of pies. Creativity is favourable because new creative enterprises find new ways to make premium profits in premium cutting edge markets and also generate the most potent new positive externalities. Diversity is important because it makes a region more secure to changes in consumer habits or economic shocks. Diversity also allows for unforeseen possible enterprises to come into existence. Creativity is proactive in searching for new sources of profit and positive externality. Diversity is more responsive in that it covers more eventualities.

> "Another blind spot in economics is its inability to understand the importance of diversity for economic growth. ... a diversity of activities with increasing returns—maximising the number of professions in an economy—is the basis for the synergy effects which lead to economic development. ... Secondly, modern evolutionary economics points to the importance of diversity as a basis for selection between technologies, products and organisational solutions, which are all key elements in an evolving market economy." (Reinert, p. 256).

The question remains as to whether creativity and diversity cause positive externalities, or whether they are caused by positive externalities. The answer is that both are generally true, but if an area is observed to be more creative and diverse in its business ideas and output than other similar areas, it is probable that this is because the activities of present enterprises are leading to new avenues of possibility. This is precisely the kind of positive externality that is so important in prosperous and robust economic development. Most new enterprises or product ideas do not just appear from the abstract genius of totally original thinking, but are the results of a path-dependent trail leading from a previous enterprise or product, often unforeseen and even often accidental. There are hundreds of examples of inventions that have only come into being as lucky accidents during efforts to solve other objectives or problems. In order for these lucky accidents to occur, people within organisations must be undertaking the original activities from which this diversion emanated in the first place. Reinert talks about seventeenth-century Netherlands as follows:

> "Knowledge developed in one sector would 'jump' to apparently unconnected sectors, proving the point that new knowledge is created by linking previously unconnected facts or events. Diversity per se came to be understood as a key ingredient in economic growth, and this diversity was not to be found in agricultural communities, where people tended to produce the same things."... "To the contemporary observers, it seemed clear that innovations and affluence were the results of the many windows of opportunity for invention outside agriculture, the falling unit costs of production and the increasing returns in urbane city activities, the extent of division of labour and the many different professions creating affluence as a product of synergies ... It is as if these theorists said: if you wish to estimate the wealth of a city, count the number of professions found within its walls" (Reinert, pp. 94 & 95).

This view of capitalism as a system of unintended consequences is why space enthusiasts justify extravagant space projects by noting the unforeseen positive externalities, such as the invention of the non-stick frying pan, and why Formula One enthusiasts claim credit for developments later used in ordinary cars. Likewise, the history of the development of medical drugs is full of stories of unforeseen outcomes. Businesses and individuals who succeed in one project are more likely and more able to make an attempt at a second project. The trail of progress started out by the participation in one industry can lead to unforeseen applications and developments in another. This process may include experimentation and failure along the way, which is financed and subsidised by the initial core business enterprise. Developing countries have a large advantage in being able to make use of the investment, experimentation and application of technology and innovation by rich countries that have already born the costs. This factor may contribute to the catch-up of recent developing countries like Korea and now China being so much more intense than the initial growth of the established rich countries.

The well-known key developments of Britain's industrial revolution in the 1700s and 1800s were characterised by one invention being necessitated and instigated by a bottleneck caused by a previous invention. These bottlenecks created a momentum that rewarded and focused the minds of the successful innovators of the time. This era proved the adage that necessity is the mother of invention. Again, the application of practical minds to practical three-dimensional problems produced outcomes that planning committees or academic business theorists could never have envisaged and realised. The practical functioning of one organisation, for example a new weaving factory, is a positive externality in that it can be the working laboratory to generate study and improvement for the benefit of subsequent organisations. The methods and ideas of the massive assembly lines of the first Ford motor factory were in small part a positive externality of observing the methods and practices of the massive 'disassembly' lines of the slaughter and meat processing plants of Chicago. The meat processors never considered this value that their working methods had, other than it worked well for them, and certainly Henry Ford would not have felt the need to rewarded them a slice of his own subsequent profits. This example highlights how unpredictable and diverse positive externalities can be. It further highlights the point that there is no theoretical substitute for learning by practical imitation and practical experimentation. In order to diversify from A to B, you have to be first at least doing A.

> "Nor were such efforts limited to men of scientific training. Indeed, one of the most remarkable features of technical advance in the eighteenth and early nineteenth centuries [in Britain] was the large proportion of major innovations made by ingenious tinkerers, self-taught mechanics and engineers ... In many instances the term *experimental method* may be too formal and exact to describe the process; *trail-and error* [original italics] may be more apposite. But a willingness to experiment and to innovate penetrated all strata of society, including even the agricultural population, traditionally the most conservative and suspicious of innovation." ... "But even more industrial advance resulted from the empirical experiments of the manufacturers of soap, paper, glass, paints, dyes, and textiles, as they sought to cope with shortages of raw materials. It is likely that in the eighteenth century chemists learned as much from the industrial users of chemicals as the latter benefited from chemical science."

> "The engineering industry, [in Britain] a creation of the late eighteenth century, can trace its roots in all three of the industries just mentioned. The textile industry needed machine builders and machine menders, the iron industry

produced its own; and the coal industry's need for efficient pumps and cheap transport resulted in the development of both the steam engine and the railway. Railways, as suggested in the previous chapter, constituted the most important new industry of the nineteenth century. They were especially important for both their forward and backward linkages to other industries. Moreover, as a result of Britain's pioneering role in the development of railways, the foreign demand in both Europe and overseas for British expertise, material, and capital provided a strong stimulus for the entire economy. Similarly, the evolution of the ship building industry from sail to steam propulsion, and from wood to iron to steel construction, was another potent stimulus." (Cameron pp. 167 & 182 & 225).

e) Economies of Scale

Finally, the dimension of economies of scale when applied to the first three types of positive externality listed above provides a further type of positive externality. Economies of scale is a concept similar to that of increasing returns to scale, which is central in Reinert's book. Reinert talks of one of the first iconic examples of a manufactured product enjoying a large benefit from economies of scale, Henry Ford's Model T car.

> "One day in January 1914 he doubled the wages of his factory workers to $5 a day ... The key point here, however, is that the barriers to entry created by the combination of technical change (innovation) and economies of scale (increasing returns) made possible a huge jump in nominal wages in this particular industry, while, at the same time, the price of cars continued to fall." ... "At the core of colonial policy is the fact that industries with such productivity explosions are not allowed in colonies." (Reinert, pp. 103 & 129).

This win-win example suggests the essence of development in a nutshell. It highlights one of the main advantages Reinert proposes that manufacturing industry has over agricultural and other commodity type sectors; this being the freedom from the chains of diminishing returns. Usually, a factory process can produce extra units without constraint and with falling marginal costs. This is in contrast to most agricultural or commodity type activities which quickly hit natural environmental constraints and do not enjoy the scale savings found in making more use of automation and machines.

> "The growth of manufacturing activities broke the vicious circles of diminishing returns, creating what was for a very long time the exclusive privilege of cities: increasing returns". (Reinert, p. 74).

The contrast between the increasing returns to scale typically found in manufacturing and the diminishing returns to scale typically found in agriculture and commodity production is the backbone concept of Reinert's book and a central positive externality in this analysis.

> "Countries specialising in supplying raw materials to the rest of the world will sooner or later reach the point where diminishing returns set in. The law of diminishing returns essentially says that when one factor of production has been produced by nature—as in farming, fishing or mining—at a certain point adding more capital and/or more labour will yield a smaller return for every unit of capital or labour added. Diminishing returns fall into two categories: *extensive* (when production is extended into inferior resource bases) and *intensive* (when more labour is added to the same plot of land or other fixed resource). In both cases, productivity will diminish, rather than increase, as the country increases its production. Natural resources are available in different qualities: fertile and less fertile land,

good or bad climates, rich or poor pastures, mines with high or low grades of ore, rich or less rich fisheries. To the extent that these factors are known, a nation will use the best land, the best pastures and the richest mines first. As production increases with international specialisation, poorer and poorer land and mines will be brought into production. Natural resources are also potentially non-renewable: mines can be emptied, fish population may be exterminated and pastures ruined by overgrazing." (Reinert, p. 108).

Of course, the benefits emanating from an economy of scale are usually most obvious when they are not externalities, but instead are benefits able to be captured within the same organisation. But there are equally important instances where the benefits of an economy of scale can be external, in that the presence of another business participating in the same marketplace or environment, allows both businesses to achieve an economy of scale in; infrastructure requirements, suppliers, common inputs or marketing. The production of good A may provide an economy of scale to the production of good B, whether they happen within the same business with one owner, or within two neighbouring businesses with two owners. This ownership distinction matters when considering the micro behaviour of firms regarding their investments and profits, but it may not matter for our purposes here, because we are interested in the generation of positive externalities alone, irregardless of how they are achieved or captured. The successful achievement of a business trading and making good returns, can then produce the positive externality of having the size and security to take the risk of supporting a new side venture. The inherent risks and costs of a new enterprise can draw on the financial security and existing resources of an established organisation, drastically cutting the costs of innovation.

Using the example of infrastructure, we have established that the more customers an infrastructure project has, the better value for money that the infrastructure provides. Secondly, using a skills example, if the demand for the specialist skill of an engineer comes from 20 businesses rather than two businesses, then it is more viable for one such person or business to locate in the local area and work in a more specialised manner. Thirdly, with many businesses in one area, it is more likely that more diverse and proficient networks will become established, and generate a greater choice of suppliers and service providers being available to fulfil any future needs that the business has. This will provide a greater variety of potential business contacts, and thus a greater number of people and organisations at the end of the phone ready to do business and help with any foreseeable eventuality.

As discussed earlier, the kind of trade that produces positive externalities is not inherently more profitable than trade that produces no positive externalities, as by definition the benefits of the externalities cannot be captured by the owners. Both types of trade rely on people with money to invest, moving resources into wherever they can get the most return, which is the equalising factor that produces equilibrium in economic theory. However, the values of costs and returns within a certain enterprise may include so much sunken investment, overhead and fixed costs as to make the minimum level of output required to break even very large. This would be an effective barrier to all entrants who could not get together the required finance and be confidant about maintaining the scale of production required right through the supply chain and on to the final sale.

Further Evidence for the Existence of Positive Externalities

a) The Costs and Benefits of the Factors of Production Rise

This is the most obvious sign of economic development on a basic level, but not necessarily the strongest point in this argument regarding positive externalities. The rising of rewards and returns for the factors of production suggest that there is a higher demand for their employment, which further suggests the 'thriving' or 'prosperous' local economy associated with economic development. However, the cost and rewards of the factors of production rising in a certain area could be due to the influence of one large enterprise or industry which does not produce enough of the right kind of positive externalities for a broadly prosperous economic future. This is in contrast to our suggested model of the many smaller enterprises producing a more diverse economy.

Consider the example of a town that had become part of the gold rush of the mid-1800s in the United States. This town undoubtedly would have experienced a rise in the costs and rewards of factors of production during that time, even in areas of business not directly related to gold. But as the gold, or hope of gold, was being exhausted, there were probably no useful positive externalities being deposited into the local business community, and when the mining and prospecting ceased, no foundation for continued enterprises of widely-traded goods remained. The existence of all the money and activity may well have encouraged an increase in saloon bars, hardware stores and banks, but as soon as the primary source of the wealth drawn from gold leaving the town dried up, these businesses could not survive on their own. The saloons, hardware shops and the banks were service-type enterprises, serving only the local community, and they relied on the excessive population and its excessive demand, which was based on their town's lucrative gold trade. To prevent the economic collapse of the community after gold prospecting slowed, it was alternative businesses of the widely traded type of goods that could pull in money from outside the area that was needed, instead of another enterprise to serve the local population. The entrepreneurial energy and knowledge that the gold rush town may have developed through sectors of its population did not lead onwards to other avenues of business, but instead led to an economic cul-de-sac that finished the town when the gold rush ended.

After the gold rush ended, the town had likely accumulated some admirable infrastructure, skills and networks of an equal quality to other, more diversely employed towns of the same size. But the nature of this business, around which their town had developed, had no adjoining avenues into which to move after the end of the gold rush. The development of positive externalities caused by the gold rush was mostly only useful specifically to the gold industry, and was not transferable or attractive to other industries, and was indeed mostly worthless when the gold industry dried up. The economic activity of gold prospecting, mining and selling left behind exceptionally poor and narrow externalities.

Many oil producing states suffer from these types of issues, as their wealth and development is focused heavily on oil production, and they have therefore not developed the complex and multi-faceted economies which other rich countries have. This should not necessarily be interpreted as the poor judgement or idle complacency of the oil-rich nations, because in fact the dominance of oil in their trading relations has often made it very difficult to diversify. This is because the oil industry's size and export value dictate that the country's currency becomes more valuable in exchange compared to its trading partners, making its exports relatively expensive abroad. The oil industry's presence also pushes higher wage and other factor costs, further making other exports using these factors uncompetitive from the outset (the Dutch Disease[3]). The response to this weakness can be seen in

---

[3] Note to non-economists: The term Dutch disease was coined by observing the problems the Dutch economy faced when it discovered and exported large values of natural gas. Because large amounts of

Saudi Arabia's long-term conservative attitude towards its oil reserves, and Dubai's quest to productively use its oil income to aggressively develop itself into a regional tourist and knowledge-based services centre.

Thus, the real test of whether an area has benefited from positive externalities should be not just a rise in the rewards and costs of the factors of production, but also a rise that was not dependent on a narrow base of an industry that is limited in its future, or vulnerable to change. The best positive externalities create alternative opportunities that fan out from the original enterprise to broaden into other markets, which in turn make the area's development more responsive to change and less vulnerable to economic shocks, including changes in technology and consumption habits.

b) Regional Specialisation

> "Far from being a few venture capital companies or semiconductor producers, Silicon Valley is a densely interwoven network of universities, law firms, venture

---

foreign currency were earned from the exported gas, the naturally equalising market mechanisms of free currency exchange rates made the Dutch currency stronger – in other words, worth more relative to other currencies. This was due to its new-found demand from other countries in that the currency was needed by them to purchase the Dutch gas. The wealth, including tax revenue generated by the gas, was a positive force upon Dutch wealth and standard of living, maintaining or increasing average wages. This meant other exporting businesses were simultaneously affected by a drop in competitiveness of their exports due to the currency being stronger abroad, and a home economic environment in which prices and wages are buoyed up by the earnings of the natural resource exporting industry. The theory shows how the discovery and exporting of a natural resource can seriously harm or prevent other exporting sectors within the same economy.

capitalists, R&D centres, local government officials, major companies, and small start-ups. In some measure, all depend on each other. Being competitive, therefore, requires just as much attention to the key interrelationships as to the single elements themselves" (Prestowitz, p. 268).

In Britain, as in other countries, areas and cities are known for what they used to specialise in making in the recent and distant past. This is related, to varying degrees, to the natural resources or strategic position of the locality. But often it is a result of the natural tendency of businesses of the same industry to concentrate in an area to take advantage of each other's positive externalities and economies of scale. Therefore, the future specialisation of a whole area can be based on a pattern started by one successful business establishing itself there along time ago. In modern academia, these ideas are viewed through concepts such as cluster theory, the study of patterns between the centre and the periphery, and agglomeration and dispersion forces in economic geography (see Henderson, Shalizi & Venables).

This highlights the distinction made earlier between these widely traded goods on one hand, and businesses that supply only a local area on the other hand. The latter type of business tends to spread out, so that each moves towards the centre of its own catchment area. In the case of the widely traded goods industries, the benefit of the positive externalities provided by sharing a location with competitors, is greater than the threat of the neighbour's competition, as most customers are far away anyway. When businesses or consumers search long distances for certain widely traded goods, they tend to come to the most prolific area to choose between suppliers.

We can see a similar example at the personal level when we consider buying a new pair of shoes. To look for a new pair of shoes, one may travel to the high street in the nearest city, where there are about eight shoe shops close together to compare, whereas if one wanted a pint of milk, a short walk to the nearest shop or supermarket would be preferable. Each of the shoe shops, and even the other shops on the high street, contribute a positive externality to the other, as together they attract customers to a concentrated area where they are all within walking distance from each other. The actual phenomena of the high street is an artifice completely resting on positive externalities to maintain the cycle of high numbers of visiting customers, together with popular stores that people want to travel to in order to do comparison-type and occasional-type shopping. The high street requires a critical mass of popular stores to be present in a pleasant location and good transport links in order for it to fulfil its function at all. Therefore, although they are enemies in competition, the shops are also locked into a collusive positive externality relationship with each other to maximise their custom.

The existence of regional specialisation, where it is not based on natural resource factors or state intervention, has no other explanation except that positive externalities must be at work. Although it may be generally hard to specifically quantify the presence of positive externalities at the individual business level, the behaviour of businesses in the places they choose to locate, when seen collectively from a distance, can display the presence of positive externalities quite clearly, with *no* other explanation possible. By far the most significant example of this regional specialisation in Britain is the City of London. As a result of Britain's previous existence as the centre of a trading empire, the City has managed to maintain its position as one of the three central financial trading centres of the world, and the leader in some sectors. London has many strong attributes as a financial centre: its business-friendly and open free trading traditions, the low regulation it has maintained (perhaps too low?), and a trusted legal and financial infrastructure. The positive externalities emanating from the existence of these trading and banking organisations, have maintained a self-feeding cycle of advantage to the area, even though the economy of Britain and its non-existent empire is now only a very small part of the world economy. When investigating why international financial companies continue to maintain and expand their London presence, our positive externalities of an excellent infrastructure, a concentration of people with specific knowledge and skills, and well-established networks and contacts would undoubtedly comprise most of the answer. Even in our age of globalisation and cheap high-tech digital communication, the City's location, backed up by positive externalities, still holds sway enough to perpetuate this advantage.

Another more recent British example of a regional specialisation and the creation of a 'cluster' of speciality and expertise can be found in the North Sea oil industry near Aberdeen in Scotland. The oil exploration, extraction and transportation activities have generated and fostered a broad and deep wealth of positive externality growth in the area, with both the established large oil companies investing heavily, and with over 2,000 small businesses developing. In typical path-dependent and co evolutionary style, because the oil in the North Sea has presented many difficulties in its extraction, and because higher and higher exhaustion rates of the fields are being desired over time, the technology and innovation development has had to be so great that the region is now recognised as a world leader in these specialist areas. In fact, the cluster has evolved so successfully that the specialist services of these Scottish branches of international oil companies and the local specialist small businesses in the area, are sought and employed in other complex oil extraction locations around the world.

Consider the process of this growth of positive externalities in this region, which has led to this desirable position in a relatively short time. First, there emerges foreign expertise (primarily American) brought in by large companies, followed by an ongoing 'engine' of positive externality generation from learning by doing, skilled and very skilled people improving, sharing and moving their specialist knowledge between organisations. Subsequently, new specialist businesses have started up to supply the large general oil companies. These start-ups are often created by employees leaving the big players and hiving off to use their insider knowledge and contacts. The major oil companies then begin considering sourcing from the Aberdeen area for other international projects, as the company ecology in the sector of difficult oil extraction has become so diverse and advanced. It is no surprise that oil-based companies exist near oilfields, but to become world class and export expertise to other difficult oil extraction locations is a great achievement, typically aided by the laying down of a generation of positive externalities. It is a typical unintended consequence.

The nature of these and previously mentioned positive externalities go a long way to explaining the success of the practice of having special zones deliberately designed to create clusters of similar economic activity in certain locations. Any brief study of the benefits and characteristics of these zones, like the ones on the coast of China, now that these positive externality ideas have been introduced, will have signs of positive externalities jumping out in vivid colours. Consider the case of the early Chinese economic zone as being a desirable campsite for campers wishing to start out in an export industry, providing and concentrating all the positive externalities in one place.

At any one time, a country is wise to hope for only a finite amount of foreign and domestic investment, or to only expect to have enough resources to build a finite number of factories and new businesses. Therefore it makes sense, especially in a large country like China, to concentrate these businesses into a zone, where the positive externalities generated can be focused effectively in one area where the impact can be maximised. Like other scientific models that include circular or self-referencing formulas and acceleration factors, a critical mass often must be reached before the take-off can begin. If the export businesses concerned were spread all over the country, the positive externalities generated by the business enterprises would be dissipated and lost, where as in a concentrated and focused zone, the highest levels of positive externalities can be achieved at the quickest pace. To illustrate this situation, consider the analogy of a coal fire made up of twenty red-hot coal pieces. If each one of the coals is spread out over a stone floor, each will lose its heat and stop burning. However, if the coals are heaped together, they maintain a burning hot coal fire by collectively generating a volume of heat which meets the critical mass, or in this case critical temperature, necessary to burn.

The most widely publicised questions regarding these zones are often the immoral aspects like tax breaks in the context of poor or developing countries that cannot afford to lose precious tax income, or the overcrowded and poor living and working conditions for their workers. There is something definitely distasteful about these issues, and ideally they should be resolved. But in an optimistic interpretation, after a certain period of time, it can quietly become the business conditions created by the positive externalities that attract the businesses, not the tax breaks and cheap labour, both of which may or may not be reversed in time. To play devil's advocate and identify an alternative justification for the popularity and success of export zones does not in itself justify any bad practice, but it does present another dimension on the justification for their existence. Anti-globalisation supporters may characterise these zones as havens of capitalist exploitation, and they may be right, but the above is the other side of the argument. If successful in aiding economic development, they can be thought of as economic 'campsites' spreading the costs and concentrating the positive externalities of export business, like the coal fire retaining and maximising the economic heat.

Consider all the elements of a decision made by an international or domestic company about where to locate and invest in a new factory or other enterprise. Beyond the basic requirements of the presence of natural resources and local markets if they are relevant, and assuming that the local wages are relatively competitive, (which they nearly always are in the context of developing countries), all the other considerations would involve positive externalities. Furthermore, these positive externalities would have to have been previously 'laid down' in the area by someone else, either by the state, business or individual. As mentioned above, on the individual enterprise level, positive externalities are rarely highlighted or considered in isolation, as they are intermingled into all specific business decisions, along with other complex information about the specifics and practicalities of that business that make up such decisions. Even the most inexperienced business professional would know to consider these elements in the decision-making process, which – although perhaps called something else by them – we could recognise here as originating from a type of positive externality. Yet even the most studious and able businessperson or organisation would find it hard to put an exact financial value on these factors, and certainly would not bother to define them precisely as positive externalities. Nor would they have the ability or motivation to accurately attribute them in accountant style to existing or previous organisations. As mentioned above, examples of positive externalities are rarely formally exposed and audited, but instead form part of the mix of factors of which experienced decision-makers are instinctively are aware.

If positive externalities are difficult to highlight and objectively value at the individual enterprise level, perhaps the next best way of looking at the subject would be from the larger perspective of the region or country, as highlighted in the last section on regional specialisation. This book argues that the existence of positive externalities are the practical economic explanation of what is at the heart of more euphemistic and vague phrases that are used to describe particular regions, such as being a 'prosperous' or 'thriving' business area. Before continuing reading, take five minutes to try yourself to define in economic language what you would expect to find if someone was showing you what they claimed was a prosperous or thriving area or city. The explanation being put forward here would have the phenomenon of positive externalities as the essence of any definition, and perhaps your definition does, too, when you analyse it further. For example, as an alternative to saying an area is 'prosperous' or 'thriving,' which only tells us about the outcome of success without suggesting a cause, one could say instead: "this area has been and is presently an environment where the positive externalities generated by existing and previous business enterprises and state activity is encouraging further successful business enterprises to enter and expand. This activity is feeding an upward, positive cycle of investment, expansion and diversification, and is consequently producing various benefits to local businesses and the general population."

It is an obvious fact that a profitable, growing business is directly beneficial for an area. The distinction being made here is that it is the less visible positive externalities that enable long-term change, through creating momentum and helping future enterprises to exist, which is key. In contrast, the more tangible and obvious jobs, profit and investment of an enterprise present in an area, although positive to those directly involved in the present, may not generate change in the long term. In other words, all profitable business benefits

its participants in the present, but the special qualities of businesses that encourage positive externalities are that they produce benefits for neighbouring businesses and for the future. These benefits can accrue long after, or far away from, the original returns to the investors and the original employee's wages paid out by the business.

Which Economic Activities Produce Positive Externalities?

"Major changes in industry and strategic focus can successfully occur, but in a step-by-step evolutionary fashion, rather than through single leaps. In their classic 1990 article, 'The Core Competence of the Corporation,' C. K. Prahalad and Gary Hamel described how Canon built on its resources in its photography and lithography businesses (in particular, optics and precision mechanics) to go into the photocopier business. This move in turn created opportunities in laser printers and faxes. These opportunities required the company to build capabilities in microelectronics, which in turn enabled Canon to become a leader in digital photography, providing both cameras and printers. Over time, resources and opportunities chase each other. The path-dependent nature of resources and the co evolutionary loop between business plans and resources thus add another factor that inhibits adaptability. A firm might simply be stuck with the wrong set of resources for the direction it needs to go, and reconfiguring those resources may take more time and money than are available." (Beinhocker, p. 367-368).

"This is not to imply that those who have their vested interest in manufacturing are better or less greedy individuals than those whose vested interests lie in the production of raw materials. As always, capitalism must essentially be understood as a system of unintended consequences, and the unintended consequences of making profits from manufacturing are different from those found in nations where everybody makes their profits from raw materials."... "...shortage of food, and famines, mostly occur in countries that specialise in producing foodstuffs. ... How can this strange reverse proportionality be explained?" ... "The gales of creative destruction focus around a specific cluster of industries. These industries are located in geographical space—be it Manchester, Detroit or Silicon Valley. ... The increase in profits and real wages creates so much purchasing power that money is easily made in a whole array of businesses that would not be feasible elsewhere." (Reinert, pp. 85, 149 & 228).

A main conclusion generally made in this subject, as alluded to in the extracts above, is that it is the trade of manufacturing and medium technology goods that causes more and the best positive externalities for developing countries. Additionally, trade of outsourced services through high-tech global communications technology can also be seen to cause useful positive externalities. In contrast, commoditised raw materials or commoditised agricultural-based goods are not generally seen to produce comparable positive externalities. The domestic and trading economic activity of poor countries can then, for the purposes here, be roughly categorised into 'favourable trade' and 'standard trade' along the lines of this distinction.

While this distinction provides an adequate starting point for considering development consequences, there could be a more subtle but less technical rule of thumb which better explains the difference between these two perceived types of trade. This rule of thumb would be that favourable trade encourages business activity that may lead to something greater in the future, while the characteristics of standard trade are that it may be presently beneficial, but it leads to a development dead end somewhere down the road. This can be illustrated on a personal level by making a parallel with some career decisions. Two jobs may be very similar in their positive and negative characteristics, but one job may lead to something further, such as a more marketable skill or a promotion, which overshadows small initial differences in pay or conditions. Likewise, the existence of a new factory serving some kind of favourable trade could in the long term improve and contribute to the infrastructure, skill and knowledge levels, or networks and contacts of an area in a way that would make it more attractive for a further factory to be built.

In contrast, the developments in a specific raw material or agricultural business of what is being called here 'standard trade,' while possibly just as comprehensive and profitable, may provide no benefits and possibilities for further growth or diversification in the greater region. For example a state-of-the-art, professionally-run banana plantation will mostly only produce benefits to that industry, and in twenty years, it will likely still only be capable of producing bananas. On the other hand, a new factory in one of China's special exporting zones can use its transferable skills and resources to move or 'jump' onto different products and industries, and be the catalyst for other factories starting up in the area. A worker in this factory in China is in the first generation, no better rewarded than the banana worker in Ecuador. The factory is inherently no more or less profitable than the banana plantation, but the point is that the positive externalities of the factory may lead somewhere, whereas the banana plantation, while being both profitable and useful and by no means to be discouraged, is, in economic development terms, a dead end.

> "The production and marketing of flower bulbs in the Netherlands—although technically agriculture—share many of the characteristics listed under 'manufacturing.' Maquila-type manufacturing, on the other hand, shares many of the characteristics of 'agriculture'." (Reinert, p. 260).

While making sweeping generalisations about what kinds of trade are relatively good and not so good for a country to engage in, it is useful and revealing to consider some of the many exceptions to this general pattern. It is too easy to fall into the lazy generalisation of capitalised manufacturing equals good, and commodities equals bad. Firstly, the United States and Canada have very profitable grain exporting industries, which would seem to go against the pattern of rich countries being involved in favourable trade. It could still be claimed that this grain trade does not contribute many positive externalities into the areas producing the grain, but the scale and technological superiority of prairie-type farming makes it consistently efficient and profitable. This industry benefits from well-suited land and climate, and the historical circumstances of the young countries, which have allowed large, unencumbered fields and patterns of ownership. This is in contrast with many foreign competitors who may have inherited the patchwork of different hedges, roads, dwellings and different ownership patterns. This small-scale ownership typically characterises good land that has been farmed for many centuries in these other parts of the world. The large fields and good land of North America allow large economies of scale which has engendered the biggest and most advanced systems, machinery and technology.

The presence of a large slice of standard trade within a country does not harm the country's future, as long as it is only a proportion within a mixed and diverse economy. This simply means that while the grain brings in immediate foreign cash, which naturally helps the country's trade balance, it is other sectors of trade and domestic production with more positive externalities that are relied upon for future progress. Grain helps the trade balance, but other areas are required to maintain the two countries' technological lead and wealthy standard of living. If the United States became only an exporter of grain, the progressive and inventive theme running through

US economic success would dry up, simply because the activity of grain production produces no opportunities for diversification and innovation and no new marketable products. It only produces ton after ton of wheat. Apart from small exceptions like the development of large combine harvesters, better strains of wheat variety and other similar advancements, the industry has not and will not lead these two regions into new, diverse and unforeseen areas of production. The grain industry is not training employees in new skills and knowledge that could lead them towards starting up new businesses. The industry is not promoting infrastructure and networking contacts that can be used by other new diverse businesses. The grain farms in the region were producing grain 40 years ago, and they will be producing grain in 40 years' time, creating trade and profits thanks to the areas fortunate advantages.

Oil provides an interesting example of an industry with a variety of potent effects on a countries economy. Above, oil has already been mentioned in the context of a very positive experience of where the region around Aberdeen benefited greatly, from the positive externalities which grew up in companies specialising in deep sea oil extraction. Then in a more negative light, oil has been mentioned in the context of the 'Dutch disease', where large oil revenue can strangle at birth other possible exporting opportunities. Another point to make about oil is that because of its unique supply and demand features, oil has not suffered from the terms of trade problems that other commodities have. Due to the conservative and long-term outlook of a few big players in the oil industry, of which OPEC has been a major part, the supply of oil is controlled in order to maintain what the industry believes is a worthy price for this finite resource. Unlike commodities that can be grown and harvested, the reserves of oil are finite, and quickly become protected by becoming the property of states or large companies when they are discovered.

Whereas other commodities can suffer from oversupply caused by too many new enterprises employing or attracting too many new farmers or miners etc, the supply of oil, although very profitable in places where it is abundant, is not very accessible as a means of employment, and therefore cannot become oversupplied in the same uncontrolled way. A peasant farmer in a suitable location can reorganise his activities within a few years to grow coffee, and all the farmers in the area will continue to do this until the price they receive for coffee drops below the price of an alternative activity for their land and their efforts. But even if they are growing coffee on land sitting atop a large oil reserve, they do not have the option to diversify into oil. Given this difference in the way potential supply is available to new entrants, it is clear which of the two commodities is going to be cheap.

The contrast of oil and coffee, and further, the contrast between commodities and manufacturing, highlight the different outcomes of being involved in different economic activities. Mistakenly the free market ideology fails to recognise the difference in prospects of the region or country entering these different sectors. Reinert adds a further dimension which highlights these distinctions between sectors, or between our favourable and standard trade goods. He describes how maintaining a "less efficient" industrial sector is desirable in order to limit the scope of the diminishing returns to scale agriculture and commodity sector.

> "For resource-rich Australia, this was the key argument which prompted the country to set up an industrial sector, even if this sector would be less efficient than those of the leading industrial nations, the United Kingdom and the United States. The existence of a manufacturing sector establishes a national wage level which prevents countries from moving too far into diminishing returns, over-producing themselves into poverty and/or emptying the fish

from the ocean and the mines of ore."... "A very important effect is that the knowledge level and high cost level in industry gradually spill over, increasing the efficiency in agriculture ... at the same time as the increasing wage level makes it profitable to invest in labour-saving agricultural machinery ... Being part of the same labour market as the cities, excess labour on the farm—the younger children—will find lucrative employment in the manufacturing sector in the cities."... "The key to coherent development is interplay between sectors with increasing and diminishing returns in the same labour market." (Reinert, pp. 109, 136 & 253).

This dimension recognises that the two broad sector groupings of manufacturing, and agriculture and commodity production, share internal markets for labour, capital and land within a country and therefore one can affect the values in the other sector. This sophisticated insight of Reinert's regarding Australia reveals an important truth regarding economic development. A country's economy contains different sectors each contributing different benefits. A large commodity or agricultural sector can indeed be pulling in the bulk of the export revenue to sustain imports. But even in these types of economy, it is positive externalities generated by industrial specialisation, producing manufactured goods and high end services, which propel a country forward into real development. Positive externalities are not always easy to examine specifically or academically rewarding to study, but a convincing general case can be made for their importance.

Chapter II

Economic Activities Matter

The Logic of Industrial Policy

The last chapter proposed that positive externalities are the key to economic development. This has led into the standard assertion made here and by alternative economists like Reinert and Chang that different economic activities are dramatically qualitatively different in terms of generating economic development.

> "From the end of the fifteenth century until after the Second World War the main theme in economic policy—if not in economic theory—was therefore what we can call 'the cult of manufacturing industry.' This involved talking about 'planting' industry in the same way one would 'plant' a useful species from foreign lands. Two different institutions serving similar purposes were both established in the late 1400s; the protection of new knowledge through *patents* and the transfer of the same knowledge into new geographical areas through *tariff protection*. Both were based on the very same type of economic understanding: the creation and geographic spread of new knowledge through the instigation of imperfect competition. An indispensable part of this process of development, were the institutions that 'got the prices wrong' compared to what the market would have done if left alone ..." (Reinert, p. 88).

The basis for the logical justification of industrial policy is therefore clear, because the mechanisms within a free market economy model, would place no monetary value on any of these positive externality effects from chapter one. The investors within the free market, if left to their own devices, will fail to value the future returns of these positive externalities within certain business activities, both because these benefits will be received by other organisations, and because the rewards are far into the future. This simple logic then provides the convincing justification for states to interfere in and manipulate the decisions within the economy of their country. Just as a totally free market with no state would fail to achieve the optimum provision of other common or merit goods such as roads or law and order, the free market could equally be argued to be failing to provide the optimum provision of positive externalities to poor and developing countries.

Free market supporters generally oppose government intervention in markets, apart from their narrow list of dispensations like the common good issues noted earlier. According to Chang, when confronted with instances of countries with interventionist states developing successfully, like, for example, Japan or Korea, they quash the possibility of this model of development being reproduced in today's poor countries, claiming that first-rate economists are needed in order to enact second rate policies successfully.

> "Indeed, Professor Winter's first-best *economists* are one thing that East Asian economies did *not* have. Japanese economic officials may have been 'first-best,' but they were certainly not economists—they were mostly lawyers by training. Until the 1980s, what little economics they knew were mostly the 'wrong' kind—the economics of Karl Marx and Friedrich List, rather than of Adam Smith and Milton Friedman. In Taiwan, most key economic bureaucrats were engineers and scientists, rather than economists, as is the

case in China today. Korea also has a high proportion of lawyers in its economic bureaucracy until the 1970s. The brains behind President Park's Heavy and Chemical Industrialisation (HCI) programme in the 1970s, Oh Won-Chul, was an engineer by training" (Chang, p. 217)

What more damning proof of the misled direction of economists during the last few decades could there be than the observation that those countries that have achieved the best economic development, are those that have *not* been led by economists? Having thought about Chang's observation, consider the practical mindset of an engineer. The engineer wants to achieve successful industrialisation in his country. The engineer gets his country to embark on an industrial policy that will lead from clothes to toys to metal goods to machinery to cars. The engineer may not formally understand the exact concept of positive externalities, but he or she would recognise the way organisations and people learn and develop in order to ramp up their potential. The engineer would recognise the way one thing leads onto another. The engineer would recognise the path-dependent history of organisations that are now engaged in complex manufacturing and business processes. The engineer would not have his practical instincts contaminated by the dogmatic theories of comparative advantage and perfect competition. Instead of heeding the *theories* peddled by the evangelising economist, he would be instead *building* organisational potential for the future. The engineer's practicality and reliance on experience would inoculate him against the strange textbook world of high, pure economic theory mentioned here by Reinert:

> "Only in that strange world of economic textbooks can nomadic yak-herders without telephones and electricity suddenly compete with and supply Silicon Valley. Only in economic theory does it take the same amount of time to grow a tree as to cut it down, namely a nanosecond." (Reinert, p. 177).

One dimension of industrial policy that is more subtle than tariffs and subsidies is that of states supporting research and development. If investing in certain research and development is likely to generate opportunities and profits, but private firms are put off because the benefits are at risk of being copied and not paid for, the state can step in. The state can choose to solve this 'free rider problem' by sinking money into R & D and just letting private firms subsequently use and copy the advancements made. This approach makes sense as long as the benefits of the state expenditure mostly goes to aid domestic enterprises, as then their profits and employment will give a return on the state's outlay. If subsequently organisations from other countries try to get a free ride on the first countries' sunken research and development costs, things get more complicated. These types of issues are a semi-hidden part of international relations, and can suck in governments and international organisations like the WTO. Here begins the subject of intellectual property and technology transfer that contains many complex subjective moral and economic incentive arguments.

The massive military and space project spending of the US government has been a huge source of positive externalities. The technological developments made over the years have regularly spilled over into new enterprises and product ideas. Furthermore, the personnel from these state-sponsored industries often cross over into private commerce, providing ready-trained scientists with which to find new commercial markets and start new businesses. Countries like Japan and South Korea did, and to a lesser extent still do, embrace this concept of the government directing and exploring the most promising areas of industry and technology ahead of the private sector. These countries have all been well rewarded by positive externalities.

> "High-quality economic activities generally emerge out of new knowledge from research. Many countries therefore

invest in basic research, because it serves as a main source of innovation, even though it is often not possible to predict the results when research begins. Inventions contain important elements of serendipity, accident or results found while looking for something else." (Reinert, p. 148).

Comparative Advantage versus Industrial Policy

Comparative advantage is one of the most powerful and influential economic principles, and is at the very heart of the controversial arguments surrounding free trade theory. It is this slightly counter-intuitive theory of comparative advantage that is the basic first line of defence of the free market supporter in the face of any threat of perceived economic ignorance. This concept proposes that, although rich country A (Germany) is more efficient than poor country B (Thailand) at producing two types of goods, for example cars and clothes, it is still an advantage for both countries to specialise. This is because Germany, in our example, is likely much more efficient at producing cars, whereas it is only slightly more efficient at producing clothes. Therefore, it is more efficient for Germany to spend all of its resources making cars, at which it is, comparatively to Thailand's different abilities, more efficient. Therefore, although a German clothes factory could produce more clothes per man-hour than Thailand, it should not produce clothes, but instead cars, where it could produce far more value per man-hour.

Assumptions made regarding this subject can be eloquently proven mathematically, and provide a robust scientific argument for the benefits of free trade, as it can be proven that if left alone, markets will find this type of comparative advantage on their own (the 'invisible hand'). The free market will, without intervention, naturally encourage Germany to make cars and export them to Thailand, and Thailand will likewise be encouraged, through the market mechanisms, to export clothes to Germany. This is the opposing side of the basic, well-worn debate that is one of the core historical and contemporary arguments within economics. The debate is between the merits of industrial policy, which aims to capture positive externalities for the future, and the merits of free trade in following the existing comparative advantage of the present. The section below in chapter four discussing five instances of countries that have developed successfully emphasises a pattern that clearly supports the industrial policy and 'future' side of the argument. Although the mathematical science of comparative advantage supports the higher wisdom of the free market in any given *static* situation, the broad narrative sweep provided by history, in contrast, seems to reward the *dynamic and far-sighted* ambition of industrial policy.

Comparative advantage and other trade theories admirably explain the snapshot of optimum rewards of different players in the game at any one point in time. But the successful examples of harnessing industrial policy have, throughout history, captured and *changed* the comparative advantage of successful countries. This is back to the chicken and egg problem. Rich countries may well be following their comparative advantage now in being advanced, but it is argued they got to this position not by following it but by managing to change it. The proposal of the alternative economists is that comparative advantage brilliantly explains a country's *present* route to optimum profitability, but an industrial policy route can positively *reshape* a country's future.

> "This simple but powerful principle—sacrificing the present to improve the future—is why the Americans refused to practise free trade in the 19th century. It is why Finland did not want foreign investment until recently. It is why the Korean government set up steel mills in the late 1960s, despite the objections of the World Bank. It is why the Swiss did not issue patents and the Americans did not

> protect foreigners' copyrights until the late 19th century. And it is, to cap it all, why I send my six-year-old son, Jin-Gyu, to school rather than making him work and earn his living." (Chang, p. 211).

Chang also notes the irony in Thomas Friedman's use of the Lexus brand in the title of his famous book, when the Lexus/Toyota enterprise was created largely as a result of the Japanese government's market-interfering industrial policies, directly counter to the policies Friedman argues for.

> "Today Japanese cars are considered as 'natural' as Scottish salmon or French wine, but fewer than 50 years ago, most people, including many Japanese, thought the Japanese car industry simply should not exist. … Had the country donned Friedman's golden straitjacket early on, Japan would have remained the third-rate industrial power that it was in the 1960's…[and] would not be exporting Lexus …" (Chang, p. 20-21).

Related to this theme of the contrast between the optimum present and the possibilities of the future, in one chapter of his book, Chang records some surprising contemporary historical quotes and observations made about the culture and character of different nations. He does this to effectively convince us that it is the economic opportunities of a nation which can shape its economic culture, and not the other way around.

> "Having toured lots of factories in a developing country, [Japan in 1915] an Australian management consultant told the government officials who had invited him: 'My impression as to your cheap labour was soon disillusioned when I saw your people at work. No doubt they are lowly paid, but the return is equally so; to see your men at work made me feel that you are a very satisfied easy-going race who reckon time is no object. …"' … "In his 1903 book,

Evolution of the Japanese, the American missionary Sidney Gulick observed that many Japanese 'give the impression ... [Chang's gap in text] of being lazy and utterly indifferent to the passage of time.' Gulick was no casual observer. He lived in Japan for 25 years (1888-1913), fully mastered the Japanese language and taught in Japanese universities." (Chang, p. 182).

Chang shows other historical examples of the negative cultural stereotyping of other countries, but it is perhaps the Japanese examples which are most surprising. This is because the contemporary cultural stereotype of the Japanese worker as the hard working, ambitious and future planning company man contrasts with the above quotes from history. Chang's point about the economic culture of a country *being created by* the economic environment is a strong one, and he effectively questions some of the cultural explanations for economic failure that free market supporters are reviving to deflect from the obvious instances of the failure of their ideology.

> "Few economists tell their children that they might as well start a career washing dishes, where they might have a 'comparative advantage', rather than seek a career as a lawyer or medical doctor, because factor-price equalisation is just around the corner." (Reinert, p. 25).

As Reinert suggests, most people do not encourage their children to settle and commit themselves to their present optimum comparative advantage activity. Instead, most parents encourage their children to attend education in order to change their comparative advantage, and not submit to an infinite continuation of the present, which would crystallise them in their present circumstance. The parent forgoes the optimum free-market income the child could earn and contribute to the family, and instead as a family, and in most countries as a community, we encourage children to continue in education. The insinuation of this dishwashing example is directed at the advice given to poor countries to specialise in what was helping to keep them poor already, namely agricultural produce and commodities. The cynical observation could be that if a country is established as a 'developed country,' it naturally seeks to crystallise the present division of labour, and retain the more positive externality-producing areas of production for itself.

The Creation of Maximum Opportunity Instead Of Maximum Capital

> "Basic economic theory would suggest that in the societies that are short of capital, the returns on capital would be high, and this would attract an inflow of private capital. ... But what about the bottom billion? ... The biggest capital flows are not going to the countries that are most short of capital; they are bypassing the bottom billion. Top of the league for investment inflows has been Malaysia, a highly successful middle-income country. The only substantial inflows of private investment to the bottom billion have been to finance the extraction of natural resources..." (Collier, p. 87-88).

> "Standard economics tends to see development as a process largely driven by accumulation of investments in physical and human capital. As we have seen, standard economic theory underlying today's development policies is generally unable to recognise qualitative differences between economic activities."... "Viewing capital per se as the key to growth, loans are given to poor nations with productive/industrial structures that are unable to absorb such capital profitably. Interest payments often exceed the rate of return on investments made." (Reinert, pp. 247 & 249).

> "The IMF displays one of the classic symptoms of planner's disease: in many countries, it keeps doing the same thing over and over again to reach a never-reached objective. The repetition itself shows the failure of previous attempts at 'short-term stabilisation' ... Repeated lending also does nothing to make the debt repayable, as debt keeps mounting without countries becoming more able to service the loans." (Easterly, p. 202).

The general label for the type of economic system in which a majority of the world lives is capitalism. This label has arisen partly to denote the contrast to the alternative for most of the last century, which were examples of state-led systems aspiring to communism. In contrast to communism, where state planners allocate investment based theoretically on what they believe is in the interests of the entire country, in capitalism, capitalists are only motivated by the rewards they receive. Therefore, it is these capitalists who partially direct the economy and shape the future. They invest to receive the highest reward and therefore, according to capitalist market theory, have chosen through the invisible hand to efficiently put the money where it can be most valuably employed. The free market ideology maintains this supremacy of the return on capital as the guiding light of economic behaviour, and defers to ground level out of the government's hands, the important decisions of where to invest the finite capital available in any economic environment. In this ideology, the best use of resources, and the most profitable use of resources will naturally be the same. The free market ideology proposes that comparative advantage will be derived from the relative price and abundance of the different factors of production, with poor countries initially having an abundance of cheap labour, and then, during the process of retaining maximised profits and savings, will *hopefully* graduate into becoming ever more capital rich.

It is therefore the process of following maximised profits and savings, in order to achieve maximum capital accumulation, which is the basis of development in the free market ideology. The model assumes that the main driving factor of development is retained profits and savings, and therefore assumes capital to be the key finite and immobile resource. In contrast it could be argued that, in the situation of a poor country trying to develop, it is not finite capital that holds back its progress, but finite promising business opportunities. Arguably the problem is the lack of environments with attractive positive externalities to enable businesses, and not the lack of start-up capital to fund business. The capital requirements of a developing country are small compared to the volume of capital in world markets, so if the reasonably safe and lucrative opportunities were present, billions could be diverted and channelled quite quickly.

> "Because we perceive capital as the source of growth, rather than technology and new knowledge, we send money to a pre-manufacturing Africa, capital that cannot be profitably invested. ... As both the conservative Schumpeter and the radical Marx agreed: capital is sterile without investment opportunities that are essentially products of new technology and innovations."... "Developing countries are given loans they cannot profitably utilise, and the whole process of financing becomes akin to that of chain letters and pyramid games." (Reinert, pp. 67 & 124).

> "Despite its extensive, and often strict, controls on foreign investment, the US was the largest recipient of foreign investment throughout the 19th century and the early 20th century—in the same way strict regulation of TNCs in China has not prevented a large amount of FDI from pouring into that country in recent decades.

This flies in the face of the belief by the Bad Samaritans that foreign investment regulation is bound to reduce investment flows, or, conversely, that the liberalisation of foreign investment regulation will increase foreign investment flows," (Chang, p. 94).

The subject of investment and the pros and cons of FDI must all be considered through the lens of positive externalities. The questions of retained profits, wage rates, conditions, tax incentives, capital investment or pricing of inter-company component trade, all become subservient to the key question: does the *economic activity contribute positive externalities* to the environment in which it is located? If a factory has all its components shipped in, no local company supplier relationships, and low transferable skills given to its assembly staff, the lack of positive externalities make that FDI not that useful. This would still be the case however morally progressive the company's ethos seems to be, or however well paid the employees. Alternatively, the greediest, most corrupt and ruthless multinational company, in our capitalist system of unintended consequences, could be laying down useful positive externalities that are invaluable to a poor country's future development. Every case must be judged by its own merits within the framework of positive externalities, and not by perceiving some other measure such as capital spending or ethical appearances. This discretionary attitude to FDI reflects the Korean attitude when they were developing.

> "The Korean government heavily controlled foreign investment as well, welcoming it with open arms in certain sectors while shutting it out completely in others, according to the evolving national development plan." ... "... Korea was one of the least FDI-dependent countries in the world until the late 1990s, when the country adopted neo-liberal policies." (Chang, pp. 14 & 95).

The Different Needs and Character of the Pioneer versus the Emulator

For its detractors, one of the main weaknesses of industrial policy is the poor ability of the state to pick and manage 'winners.' The state can seem cumbersome and inept compared to private enterprise in searching out and replicating business opportunities. But after a few decades observing the results of free market policies in action in some countries, the choice seems to be between an industrial policy route which often does not work, and a free market policy that will never work. A few untypical examples like Hong Kong, which had a unique role and location, have developed through relatively free trade, but few other examples bear up to scrutiny.

One key argument must be that often the gulf of advantage and capability between an agricultural or commodity-based economic environment, and the requirements of a desirable manufacturing enterprise is so large that the small steps of private, free-market capital would never make that dangerous leap. It is easier to get private capital to follow short steps towards a slightly new alternative promising business plan, than it is to get a business to strike out on its own with a radically different business plan and be the very first 'pioneer.' New business ventures are inherently risky. Therefore investors are wise to make small careful steps that build on or replicate existing activities, and not solo radical changes of direction into the unknown.

Economic development and progress are about a country entering into new economic activities. However, it is evident that when considering whether an economic activity is 'new,' there is an important distinction to be made between whether the activity is completely new and original to the whole economic world, or just new to that particular country.

It could be argued that distinguishing between these two types of 'newness' allows for different assumptions to be drawn about the best way to proceed. The first type of newness is the absolute originality of brand new technology and/or brand new innovation contained within the new business enterprise from a *global* perspective. The degree to which the economic activity is new in this sense depends on the difference or *leap* between what that business is doing and what its closest rival in that *international* market is doing. We will call a business partaking in this kind of newness a 'pioneer.' The other type of newness referred to is how big a difference or leap a new business enterprise is, from the existing economic activity *within that environment*. We will call a business taking part in this kind of newness an 'emulator.'

Given these two types of newness, the pioneer and the emulator, the following assertion can be made about a business in a developing country. It is possible that a business in a developing country is making an investment into an enterprise which is a big leap in terms of the national economic ecosystem in which it operates, but that it is still a fairly unoriginal enterprise model from an international perspective. It would be a large leap for the business actors involved, because there would be no positive externalities or synergies or agglomerations within the country's economic environment to foster and nurture this radically new activity. It would be an unoriginal model of enterprise internationally, because it is being already done and has been done in other developing countries. For example, a T-shirt factory in a developing country with only agriculture is a large leap, but into an unoriginal model of enterprise. It is new to them, but not a new economic activity. This emulation combination would be more disposed to an effective industrial policy, as otherwise the private capitalist entrepreneurs would not consider the great risk a viable one, as they would be novice new entrants trying to take on strong incumbent international producers.

In contrast, a new type of mobile phone technology in a rich country could be a relatively small leap in economic activity within the technologically advanced environment, but creating a pioneering new and original service or product never seen before in the world. This later combination would be more disposed to the diversity and creativity of free market enterprise, as state planning would be too slow and unresponsive. Therefore in this case a targeted industrial policy would be a clumsy blunt tool with which to attempt to produce such a complex outcome.

> "Innovation is generally not as mysterious or idiosyncratic as it is so often portrayed, the work of an isolated, driven, lonely genius. Rather, it happens in clusters, groups, or communities of innovators busying around some major, enabling scientific development that is well known globally. The innovations that open commercial applications happen within these small communities of innovation and slosh around its constituent people, institutions, and firms. No one can really know who will hit the winning combination, but it is a fair bet that someone will, most likely more than one. ... That is why venture capital firms have such redundant portfolios: one firm in this charged space will likely hit it; we just can't know which." (Cohen & DeLong, p. 133).

It is argued here that the internationally pioneering blue skies investments of rich countries is a complex decision process better suited to the risk spreading, searching, diversifying and responsive qualities of private enterprise. In contrast, the first steps into well-trodden clothing production or basic manufacturing sectors are inherently a process of emulation, which could arguably be more successfully encouraged through state assistance and planning. The approach towards the subject of technology and innovation within this section are influenced by Eric D. Beinhocker's book *The Origin of*

Wealth, although these are not his conclusions. In one part of his book, he illustrates the possibilities and evolution of the economic world as being like a model landscape with hills of improving competitiveness and valleys of un-viability and extinction. By populating this terrain with individually autonomous actors with simple, self-preserving behaviour, he is able to show how their individual self-interested decision making leads them towards greater progress, without any overall co-ordination or planning.

> "In order to search the landscape, we might first pick a random starting point and then use the following simple rule: take a step in a random direction; if the step led you up, stay there and take another random step. If not, return to where you were before and try again. You can imagine that if your starting point were down in a valley and you were following this rule, you would initially wander the valley floor in random directions. But eventually you would find a path up and pretty quickly scale the nearest peak. This rule is called an *adaptive walk*. While the adaptive walk is efficient at climbing individual peaks, it has an important limitation: once you reach the top of a peak, you stop and are stuck on a local maximum. There might be a much higher peak just a short way over the valley, but you will never find it, because you would have to go down first to get to it. The adaptive walk could even get stuck on a molehill right in the middle of a field of Everests." (Beinhocker, p. 208).

This blind searching behaviour of the "random walk" could be recognised as an important component of an optimum strategy in the unknown environment of the private capitalist pioneer, who was blindly searching the frontiers of technology and innovation for globally new business strategies or products. But the image of being "stuck on a molehill right in the middle of a field of Everests" could be interpreted as an argument in favour of industrial policy if, as an 'emulator', you are not blind, but you *know*, by observing other more developed countries, where the "Everests" are around you. Remaining active only in standard trade commodity and agricultural goods production could be your country's "local maximum" or "molehill". It would have to be industrial policy that supported you or your business while you climbed off your molehill and travelled across the unprofitable valley towards the base of a higher mountain, or better economic activity.

Easterly's favourite distinction in his book *The White Man's Burden*, as can be surmised from the chapter headings, is the distinction between "planners and searchers". He appears to be broadly in favour of a free market and comparative advantage, and this distinction of the planner and the searcher could be considered his shorthand for the industrial policy versus comparative advantage and free trade debate. In his analysis, bottom up searchers are preferable, which reflects the fact that although he is effectively critical of the economic orthodoxy, he remains mainly a free market believer. In agreement with Easterly, the assertion could be made that private enterprise searchers are better at blindly finding pioneering originality and profitable niches within complex economic systems. In contrast, however, perhaps the bold leaps made possible by state-planned industrial policy are required when making the distinct and radical changes of economic activity necessary for an emulation plan. Searchers could be argued to be better at small leaps of originality in complex environments, while planners could be preferable for large leaps in developing countries into industries *which are new to them, but not at all original* in their business enterprise models.

Easterly has to stretch his assertion of searchers being better than planners when he talks about Japan after WWII.

"... the Americans had left untouched the large banks that had become their nerve centres. The American occupation preserved and perhaps even reinforced the Japanese bureaucracy that was to implement Japan's peculiar state-managed capitalism. Public and private Japanese searchers soon found the consumer electronics, automobile, steel, and other industries that would fuel Japan's extraordinary post-war export boom." (Easterly, p. 302-303).

Having read about Japanese successes through other writers, a few points stand out for me in this passage. Firstly, describing Japanese banks as "nerve centres" seems an attempt to make them appear primarily responsive in nature to their client enterprises, where as other descriptions of the period show them to be primarily proactive in nature, imposing plans on their client organisations that dictated where or which markets and sectors they should be in. Also, Japan's "peculiar state-managed capitalism" *was* the exception rather than the norm for a country's economic behaviour, as its growth was exceptional also. It shares these exceptional qualities with the *exceptional* way Britain's state went to enormous lengths to build a dominant Royal Navy and trading empire, and the exceptional way America was once one of the highest tariff countries in the world. Even more like the "exception" of Japan is the way Korea followed a very similar "exceptional" route out of poverty, heavily reliant on state planners also. China is presently an exception, as has been described, because it certainly is not a model of free market behaviour.

After this, Easterly writes that Japanese searchers *"found"* the consumer electronics, automobile, steel and other industries that would fuel Japans extraordinary export boom. If a bank that is holding the purse strings to your future is directing your organisation towards producing in a particular market, and you then labour industriously within this market for years before achieving successes, and furthermore you make a loss and not a profit for many years because your products and methods are not competitive, would you describe yourself as having "*found*" this market when eventually you became successful? The key companies in Japan's post-war boom had not been only searching – they had been pushed by planners in many key instances. The majority of Easterly's examples of searchers being better than planners in development situations are sound, and I am perhaps unfairly singling out only this subject, but trying to apply this analysis to the infamous case of Japanese industrial policy could be argued to be a step too far.

As stated in the introduction, industrial policy is not presented here as the panacea and answer to all questions, but its historical significance and continued potency in many contemporary situations must be emphasised in order to reach an accurate understanding of our economic world.

PART TWO

Business is War

CHAPTER III

The Conflict of Trade Interests

The Prize: Export-Led Growth in the Right Sectors

"The loss of agricultural activities hurt the farmers who had produced them, but it probably didn't of itself curtail the growth process because traditional export agriculture was generally not a very dynamic sector with many opportunities for technological progress and productivity growth. However, the Dutch disease can damage the growth process by crowding out export activities that otherwise have the potential to grow rapidly. The key activities are labour-intensive manufactures and services, the sort of exporting now done by China and India." (Collier, p. 39).

"To give an example: you observe a poor part of town inhabited by people making their living by washing dishes in restaurants and shining shoes, and a rich part of the same town inhabited by stockbrokers and lawyers. ... The toolbox of that [free market] theory hardly contains any instruments with which you can observe qualitative differences between economic activities. Barred from saying that differences in earnings between shoe-shiners and stockbrokers are a direct result of inherent differences between the two professions, economists therefore come up with explanations that tend to be secondary effects of the main cause: the poor have not enough education...have not saved enough...have not innovated enough."

"The above examples all involve crony capitalism and rent-seeking behaviour which mainstream economic theory tends to abhor. However, a crucial difference separates the first example from the rest. The Filipino crony differs from the other cronies in that he gets subsidies for a raw material with diminishing returns that compete in a world market facing perfect competition. In other words, he is a Malthusian crony, leading his country down the path of diminishing returns. The others are Schumpeterian cronies, producing under what Schumpeter called historical increasing returns." ... "If we insist on abandoning industrial policy because moving away from perfect competition will cause some cronies to get rich, we have totally misunderstood the nature of capitalism. After all, capitalism *is* about getting away from perfect competition. The most important thing good business schools teach is how to escape from the situation of perfect competition that economists tend to assume." (Reinert, pp. 214 & 254).

Suggesting that positive externalities are the key to the progress and development of a country also implies that some economic activities are more desirable than others. Free market theory presumes that profits and employment created by any economic activity are inherently equally valuable. But follow a positive externality mindset and it is apparent that this equality in the eyes of the market is a naïve fruit of an inadequate ideology. Therefore, as discussed above, it is often thought desirable to adopt an industrial policy to *steer* a country towards certain economic activities. Examples of industrial policy can be thought of as consisting of two types: import substitution policies, and export-led growth policies. A country engaged in import substitution is seeking to supply only its own population and therefore can only increase its economic activity in favourable sectors in line with its modest domestic consumption. In contrast, a country that achieves export-led growth can tap into world markets and increase its output in these positive externality-generating activities exponentially. This process can accurately explain the dynamics of international contrasts in development in history. This has always been the prize in international trading, and in the next chapter, this will be illustrated by describing five examples of winners within this competitive game.

Even in one of the most open and free market business environments in the world such as Britain, these free market unfriendly ideas lurk in the economic subconscious and political shadows. It is for these reasons that loss-making car factories or advanced engineering businesses were supported in the past, and why extra fuss is made when these industries lose jobs. It is these ideas which motivate politicians to propose investments in green technology and why sectors like pharmaceuticals and bio science receive such a high profile in the business press. Although we nominally have adopted quite a free market stance as a country, we instinctively know to value aspects of our economy, even though our adopted ideology has no way of recognising this distinction.

Reinert, below, illustrates a further dimension that makes economic activities different. Not only is it desirable for a country to be engaged in an economic activity that generates positive externalities which 'spill over' into neighbouring activities, but the very best contemporary economic activities can be so desirable that they also achieve exceptional rewards for those *within* the sector. These special periods of certain economic activities are so dynamic in terms of the improvement in technology and innovation they are experiencing that they cause large productivity jumps or steep learning curves. All positive externality-generating economic activities are desirable, but certain sectors in certain periods of time are development rocket fuel. This is a further explanation as to why the type of economic activities a country is engaged in matters.

"Economic growth is activity-specific in the sense that, at any point in time, few economic activities exhibit a very sharp learning curve." ... "In 1850 15.5 work hours were required to produce a pair of standard men's shoes. Then a productivity explosion took place in shoe production, and rapid mechanisation made it possible to employ only 1.7 labour hours to produce an identical pair of shoes fifty years later, in 1900. St Louis, Missouri, in this period became one of the wealthiest cities in the USA, based on production of shoes and beer ... After 1900 the learning curve for shoes flattened out. In 1923 1.1 working hours were needed to produce the same pair of men's shoes. In 1936 0.9 hours were needed. As the learning curves flattened out, pressure on wages increased, and gradually shoe production moved to poorer regions. ... now the country imports practically all its shoes." ... "The toolbox of standard textbook economics does not contain tools to record the fact that at any time there are only a few industries behaving as shoe production did at the end of the 1800's, as car production did seventy-five years later, and as the production of mobile phones does now. This form of economic growth (that this happens only in a few industries at any point in time, ..." (Reinert, pp. 146, 137 & 139).

The Arithmetic Problem: The Ultimate Check on Development

"But there was an arithmetic problem. ... Until we earth citizens begin large-scale, interstellar trade with the planet Vulcan, global trade must balance." (Cohen & DeLong, p. 92).

Alarm bells should have already started ringing as the preceding sections were being read. The problem with this export-led, growth-based route as a hope for the widespread development of all, and not just one country, is obvious when its very nature is considered. To illustrate this problem, it is useful to hypothesise about an extreme industrial policy scenario. The more basic industrial policy of import substitution could be carried out in extreme by every country on Earth, up to the point where no trade took place in any of the areas of positive externality-producing economic activity. This would mean that only goods and services that were not deemed by governments to be important enough to protect, or which were regionally specific for climate or natural resource reasons, would be traded. This would be far worse than the present due to destroying the benefits of competition like efficiency and incentives, but essentially possible. Even if efficiency and incentives could be artificially induced, diseconomies of scale and the costs of massive duplication would cause a massive absolute cost. In this scenario, each country could change its own economy in this way without requiring any specific condition from any other country, and indeed could allow for and accommodate other countries following the exact same course of action.

In contrast, the most basic rules of economics indicate that it is technically impossible for more than a minority of countries by volume to be achieving substantial export-led growth at any one time. This is the equilibrium principle or arithmetic problem, in that demand and supply, imports and exports must inevitably match up on a world scale. In order for any one country to develop through export led growth, it needs to exist in a world economic environment that can absorb its surpluses and provide for its deficits. In terms of physical trade this would require absorbing exports of manufactured positive externality-generating goods and providing its deficit of raw materials, agricultural and commodity needs.

Recently, this inevitable imbalance in physical trade has been accompanied by a severe imbalance in financial flows, most notably regarding China. China's export-led growth stance has been so extreme that it is nowhere near reciprocating its imports with its exports in its trade with the West, and has maintained this imbalance and its low currency through lending money to the West. As China's extreme stance reveals, by definition, only a proportion of countries by trade volume can be net exporters within these positive externality-generating markets, as some countries will inherently have to be net importers. A country involved in export-led growth must relate to the rest of the world in a certain way. To enable its existence it requires that other countries as a whole form a kind of mirror image in the nature of their trade relationships. A country prospering from export-led growth can only exist in a world where all other countries collectively import more of these (usually manufactured) positive externality goods than they export. Consider the example of ten people on a remote desert island. Their best individual route to becoming well off could be to grow food for their fellow islanders to eat. But can all ten of them each produce more than they consume, each of them sell more than they buy? The answer is no. An equilibrium balance will have to evolve.

As Cohen and DeLong point out below, in recent decades the US has acted as an importer of last resort in the world trade system. With its previously relatively strong economic position and its unique advantage of being able to print the world's default currency in exchange for imports, the US has been able to enable a greater volume of export led growth activity by developing countries. China has been the biggest client of this enabling US activity, and as a direct result has now accumulated a large wedge of US debt in dollars.

> "A better, more automatic, less manipulable, and less easily distorted by corruption and rent-seeking way to accomplish the same end is for the government to concentrate on keeping the value of the currency low. Exchange-rate manipulation is a way of creating a broad-based subsidy

program that is not easily subject to the what-do-you-do-when-your-nephew-comes-calling? problem ... The developmental states that use currency-value manipulation to send their industrial sectors the message to transfer labor from near-subsistence agriculture to the industrial production of modern goods are the most successful. China, of course, has been the most extreme and the most successful example of this development strategy in recent years—in fact, it is the most successful example of large-scale economic development ever. ... The US willingness to serve as importer of last resort was an essential block of China's development strategy, based as it was on rapidly expanding production in 'modern' goods ... A policy of an undervalued currency does not, however, maintain itself ... The government must step in to offset the rise in demand for domestic currency by increasing the supply. It must print and sell the domestic currency and in the process, buy up the foreign exchange and hold it. A policy of export-led industrialisation via an undervalued currency is also a policy of massive accumulation of foreign exchange by the government." (Cohen & DeLong, pp. 76–79).

When considering a country in isolation, to follow the industrial policy route to success as described appears watertight as a tactic. But the reality is that at any one time, there are only so many areas of high-volume economic activity that are available and suitable. Few economic activities contain the right mix of high volume markets, with moderate technology and yet still a realistic chance of market accessibility. Given the finite nature of industries experiencing even modest productivity gains, just as a country realises that certain activities are desirable to enter, other countries at a similar level of economic development will likely make the same realisation at the same point in time. They may experience similar contemporary consumer trends within their own country or in their target market countries—all this while observing or learning of the same technology and innovation developments. In having similar mindsets about what type of production helps economic development, they could be expected to come to the same conclusions about what their country should be producing. They will become like graduates all applying to the same few prestigious job vacancies. In the last few decades, the US and other Western countries have augmented the opportunities for export-led development by allowing imports without reciprocal exports. But their capacity to perpetuate this state of affairs is limited and has been checked by the recent recession. The bottom line is that opportunities for export-led growth are finite, which explains why only a limited amount of development takes place across the world at any point in time. This is the ultimate check on development and world poverty relief.

The Conflict of Industrial Policy Players versus the Docile Harmony of Free Traders

> "The neoliberals were quite right to try to rein in 'industrial policy' in many of its various forms: Subsidies, undervaluation of currencies, and outright protection are at best zero-sum from a global point of view. Whenever market outcomes in industry after industry are significantly shaped by the policies of nations supporting their champions, it creates a severe system problem. The market then tilts towards a system of competitive, predatory competition between governments seeking to protect and subsidise profits and jobs at home. Overcapacity and inefficiency grow —unless, of course, some very big nations let their companies and workers be squeezed in the interest of pursuing other goals, like rallying the global West in a Cold War." (Cohen & DeLong, p. 11).

If a country changes its beliefs concerning the merits of free trade and comparative advantage, along with this would also go a fundamental shift in how that country would approach and conduct its trade relations. A country that believed broadly that the economic activities in which it engaged are key to dictating its economic potential would be inclined to manage and 'steer' its businesses. Rather than docilely accept its role in the world's division of labour as a neutral outcome, it would be inclined to promote and guard jealously the country's most positive externality-rich industries. Extrapolate this change in emphasis up to the international level, and it is easy to perceive that a world full of 'economic activities matter' and industrial policy inclined countries would be very different from a free market comparative advantage-inclined world.

Poor countries that are comparative advantage believers would support and accept the present international division of labour in a docile manner, and humbly accept their lot as producers of commodities, agricultural goods and low-tech labour-intensive manufacturing. Not only would they accept this status quo, but would consider this role to be their optimum route to achieving development through capital accumulation, based on maximum reinvested profits from businesses and maximum reinvested savings from investors. In contrast, the industrial policy alternative as put forward in the books by Reinert and Chang, and as presented above, supports the concept of different economic activities being qualitatively different, in terms of how they reward their participants. The rewards of industrial policy would represent the *maximum opportunity* to achieve positive externalities, medium-term specific sector industrialisation goals, and long-term export-led growth goals. This change in economic philosophy towards emphasising the qualitative difference between economic activities will inherently introduce at the same time the possibility that countries could become locked into conflict of interests with each other over how they trade.

The comparative advantage free trade ideologies generate a harmonious, naturally determined order, while the industrial policy and qualitatively distinct activities standpoint requires and predicts that countries will be more predatory and combative in mode. Different countries believing in the free market and comparative advantage ideology would never have any conflict of interests over which sectors they traded in, so long as their trading partners were equally 'free' and reciprocal in their trade practises. Countries' governments would not even attempt to monitor or change their exports or imports, as the invisible hand of the free market would be implicitly trusted to automatically find their comparative advantage in a conflict-free way. This contrast in approaches is illustrated by various anecdotes which describe how the Japanese government in the past knew more about the profile of parts of the American economy than that country's own government. The stance of the US government was that it was not their business to dictate what economic activity took place, but only consider the best conditions for its flourishing. The ideology suggests that the free market would automatically find for any country what its workers and businesses should be producing and what it should be exporting and importing. Free trade theory can mathematically prove how this approach maximises the wealth of the country as a whole in the present.

In contrast taking the industrial policy viewpoint, countries should not always docilely accept economic activities that are their present comparative advantage, but distort their markets in order to direct their investments and energies into sectors where they want to be. This will necessarily mean conflict of interests with other countries as they will *have to* discriminate against the exports or the domestic producers of other countries in this process. Their goods can become as 'competitive' as the government is willing to afford through subsidy and tariff, with the competing country losing trade. Once markets are no longer based on notionally unfettered competition for lowest costs, but instead slewed by state interference, then heightened sensitivities and disagreements towards trade issues is to be expected.

From an international equilibrium perspective, a country succeeding within this mode of operation has to improve its role in the international division of labour. By definition, this must require it to be able to make other countries accept this state of affairs and miss out on their own optimum opportunities to a degree. A domineering country maintaining this favourable trade relationship requires that the losing or weaker trading partners be kept in a position not in their own long-term interest, either by being dominated by some kind of power, or by the weaker trade partner capitulating. The difference between domination and capitulation, in this case, is that domination is a relationship where the absolute superior power of the winner can force the loser to take part. Capitulation, however – defined in my dictionary as "surrendering on agreed terms" – suggests that the losing party does not have to give in to the winner due to absolute power advantage, but chooses to for some other reason. The following from Reinert contains an extract from a book about President Roosevelt and details a conversation he had with Winston Churchill. It is interesting because it reveals how obvious it was to Churchill that trade domination and economic prosperity go hand in hand.

> "The American turnaround from defender of the rights of poor countries to classic imperial power is relatively recent. When in 1941 Winston Churchill used all his charm to convince President Franklin D. Roosevelt to enter the war, Roosevelt took the opportunity to vent his frustration over the historical injustice of English economic policy. Here Roosevelt's son, Elliot, tells the story of the historic meeting on a battleship off the coast of Newfoundland:

Churchill shifted in his armchair. 'The British Empire trade agreements,' he began heavily, 'are—'

Father broke in. 'Yes. Those Empire trade agreements are a case in point. It's because of them that the people of India and Africa, of all the colonial Near East and Far East, are still as backward as they are.'

Churchill's neck reddened and he crouched forward. 'Mr President, England does not propose for a moment to lose its favoured position among the British Dominions. The trade that has made England great shall continue, and under conditions prescribed by England's ministers.'

'You see,' said Father slowly, it is along in here somewhere that there is likely to be some disagreement between you, Winston, and me. I am firmly of the belief that if we are to arrive at a stable peace it must involve the development of backward countries. Backward peoples. How can this be done? It can't be done, obviously, by eighteenth-century methods. Now-'

'Who is talking about eighteenth-century methods?'

'Whichever of your ministers recommends a policy which takes wealth in raw materials out of a colonial country, but which returns nothing to the people of that country in consideration. Twentieth-century methods involve bringing industry to these colonies. Twentieth-century methods include increasing the wealth of a people by increasing their standard of living, by educating them, by bringing them sanitation—by making sure that they get a return for the raw wealth of their community.'

Thus, only sixty-odd years ago, we find the US using all its power to contest the economic theory that all countries could become wealthy no matter what they produced. The more cynical of my Latin American friends would claim that this was part of an American plot to take over Britain's position as global hegemon. I think the Marshall Plan shows there was more to it than that" (Reinert, p. 168-169, & the extract Reinert quotes from Elliot Roosevelt, *As He Saw It*, New York, 1946).

As Winston Churchill seems to understand above, successful outcomes of export-led growth policies are reliant upon other countries being dominated or capitulating to your needs. The worst outcome is an escalation of tit for tat retaliatory trade policies and tariff barriers, as competing countries fight to defend their own interests. If a country's trading partners are able to or choose to retaliate instead of capitulate, everyone loses, and its plans for export-led growth fail. Free trade economists suggest with some justification that the free trade ideology defends the wellbeing of the whole, where as industrial policy and tariffs represent the 'beggar thy neighbour' tactics of countries winning a small gain for themselves at the risk of causing a larger loss to the rest of the world system. It is worth mentioning here that this potential for deterioration in trade relations plays a large part in shaping the conclusions later. The fear of escalation inherent in protectionism points to a shift away from traditional industrial policies aimed at protecting prestigious industries and products, as these would feed international antagonisms.

The most basic example of a developing country's industrial policy is in seeking to gain advantage by undervaluing their currency exchange rate. This basic type of industrial policy is a major source of conflict in international relations, and the imbalance it has caused between China and many Western economies, most importantly the US, is the biggest issue in modern world economics. Here again, in a more harmonious spirit, free market supporters would advise that all currencies should 'float' and adjust against each other, which would reflect and not distort trade values. The deliberate holding down of your country's currency value inherently is a zero sum game at international level: it only works if your trading partners capitulate to this distorted exchange and take the hit of allowing their domestic produce to become less competitive. As the China-US example shows, China's behaviour requires capitulation from the US in tolerating China's holding of large amounts of US debt/currency reserves. As mentioned, this dynamic is a notable phenomenon in contemporary world economics and at the centre of the recent economic problems. It adds further weight to the premise that industrial policy often generates international conflict of interests, whereas free market solutions can seem more neutral.

Game Theory and the Role of the WTO

"The problem, however, is that if the other guy is doing it [industrial policy] and you're not responding in some way, you become part of his policy—a policy aimed at beating you." (Prestowitz, p. 183).

"America must restructure its economy again, and so must the world. Countries that seek to grow cannot all just continue by promoting export-led growth alone. And a United States that no longer has the money or the unshakable credibility of vast economic strength cannot for much longer be the importer of last resort to support the international system of open trade and open financial markets. The open-markets system relied not just on the much-celebrated invisible hand, but also on a system guarantor. One big economy had to be willing and able to run trade deficits to absorb others' net exports and to issue debt for others that seek safe assets to hold." (Cohen & DeLong, p. 13).

The concepts of game theory are very apt in considering international trade relationships, because the success of the export-led growth strategy depends wholly on other countries not all choosing or being able to act the same. As in the famous 'prisoner's dilemma,' the free market economists could argue that the optimum outcome for all players collectively is for them all to forego their individually optimum strategy, this being the selfish industrial policy and tariff route.

Consider the implications of the following statement: the best outcome for a country perusing positive externalities through industrial policy aimed at export-led growth is for the rest of the world to be committed to free trade. Typical to game theory, to maximise personal gain one must 'cheat' in a game where all other players naively follow the rules generally considered best for everyone. If everyone cheats, in that every country aims for export-led growth, no more than a minority of countries can succeed, and the barriers to trade could cause real negative economic effects, meaning no one succeeds.

In light of this reasoning, the WTO's remit now does not look so divisive, and a simple generic industrial policy solution to universal world development is arguably harder to perceive. However, a cynic should consider the thought that the WTO is the mechanism that is trying to stop the majority of the players of the game from cheating, but that the most powerful and capable players could be using it as a tool to increase the potential benefit of them being able to cheat themselves. As pointed out above, common to game theory the best outcome can be achieved where a player forces his competitors to follow the general interest, while he has the power and influence over the system to cheat. While this cynical conspiracy scenario theory is not flawless, the potential dynamic is there. Due to these arguments surrounding common good and tit for tat trade practices, the necessity of an organisation like the WTO existing is strengthened, but the requirement for it to be fair, even-handed, and beyond influence becomes more paramount. Unfortunately it is fair to say that this impartiality is not yet a reality within the WTO, as many accounts of WTO actions by critics can testify. There is widespread recognition among critics that the structure and execution of WTO meetings favour the richer, more powerful countries, with their armies of well-paid representatives, in contrast to the poor countries' thinly-spread staff. Poor country representatives are routinely overwhelmed by the volume of information and logistical demands of the organisation's processes, and therefore enter all negotiations at a disadvantage.

> "Many believe that it [the WTO] is little more than a tool with which the developed countries pry open developing markets. ... It is reported that, in various ministerial meetings (Geneva 1998, Seattle 1999, Doha 2001, Cancun 2003), all the important negotiations were held in the so-called Green Rooms on a 'by invitation-only' basis. Only the rich countries and some large developing countries that they cannot ignore (e.g., India and Brazil) were invited. ... the decisions are likely to be biased towards the rich countries. They can threaten and bribe developing countries by means of their foreign aid budgets or using their influence on the loan decisions by the IMF, the World Bank and 'regional' multilateral financial institutions....
>
> "Moreover, there exists a vast gap in intellectual and negotiation resources between the two groups of countries. A former student of mine, who has just left the diplomatic service of his native country in Africa, once told me that his country had only three people, including himself, to attend all the meetings at the WTO in Geneva. The meetings often numbered more than a dozen a day ... In contrast, the US—to take the example at the other extreme—had dozens of people working on intellectual property alone. ... Many more stories like this can be told, but they all suggest that

international trade negotiations are a highly lopsided affair; it is like a war where some fight with pistols while the others engage in aerial bombardment." (Chang, p. 36).

Collier presents a different view of the WTO which does not seek to defend head on its record in its dealings with poor countries, but instead deflects criticism of the organisation and reframes the debate by redrawing our expectations regarding what we should be expecting the WTO to achieve.

"What are the countries of the bottom billion doing in the WTO? It is the successor organisation to GATT, and its basis is reciprocal bargains: I open my market to you if you open your market to me. It is not an international organisation in the same sense as, say, the World Bank, the IMF, or the United Nations Development Programme. It does not have resources to disburse to countries, nor an objective that its staff must achieve with such resources. It is not a purposive organisation but rather a marketplace. The WTO secretariat is there merely to set up the stalls each day, sweep the floor each evening, and regulate opening hours. What happens is determined by the bargaining. This made some sense when bargaining was between the United States and the European Union.

"Over the years, US-EU trade in manufactures became virtually free of restrictions. The WTO brought in the emerging developing countries: India, Brazil, China and Indonesia, which have a lot to offer to both each other and to rich countries in terms of reduced trade barriers. In return they can negotiate better access to rich-country markets. But the markets of the bottom billion are so tiny that even if their governments were prepared to reduce trade barriers, this would not confer any bargaining power on them. If the US government decides that the political gains from protecting cotton growers outweigh the political cost of making American taxpayers finance a hugely expensive farm bill, the offer of better access to the markets in Chad is not going to make much difference. So far, the WTO has functioned badly. The present round of trade negotiations was termed a 'development round,' but such labels really have no possibility of content in an organisation designed for bargaining. You might as well label tomorrow's trading on eBay a 'development round.' Trade negotiators are there to get the best deal for their own country, defined in terms of the least opening of home market for the maximum opening of others. The countries of the bottom billion joined the WTO hoping to receive transfers in some shape or form, just as they do in the other international organisations such as the World Bank, and the IMF, and the United Nations. But the WTO is simply not set up to do this. As long as it is merely a marketplace for bargaining, the bottom billion have no place in it." (Collier, p. 170).

The points Collier makes above certainly throw off balance the usual critique of the WTO. It ducks the main punches by claiming a reduced "marketplace" remit and a limited disinterested input. This is in contrast to the common critical perception of it being a partisan tool of free market interests with inherent independent authority and therefore organisational responsibility for outcomes. Many critics would propose that the way the mechanisms of the WTO are designed would lead to the conclusion that *it is* a "purposive organisation" in that it seeks to generate more free trade. As far as I am aware, the tools and mechanisms of the WTO move only in one direction, like a ratchet effect, towards free trade, and they do not allow the reversal of trade liberalisations as a truly non-"purposive," "marketplace" organisation would do in theory. If two or a group of countries concerned wanted this reduced free trade "bargaining" outcome, would the WTO facilitate this reversal? Is it really an ideologically neutral "marketplace"? The passage above also confesses that the aim of countries' trade negotiators is to achieve the least opening of their own country and the maximum opening of others. This supports a common critique of free trade theory. This is that if free trade is so good, as fundamentalist free market adherents would claim, why do countries not remove their market protection laws of their own accord? Collier, however, on the whole presents a more sophisticated view than a fundamentalist free market believer would, and also the game theory analysis above provides part of the answer to this question of countries negotiating their interests as a group.

Recognising the conflict of interests present in anti free market trade policies reveals that there is a requirement for arbitration and negotiation and therefore an organisation to formalise this. It is therefore just as lazy for the left to label the WTO as a totally harmful or evil organisation, as it is naive to be a free market evangelist and swallow whole all the details of the free trade ideology. We can argue for a different WTO, but we definitely need one, and if its enemies gain support on anti free trade issues, we will need it more and not less.

Chapter IV

The Winners and the Losers

Five Examples of Winning

In asserting that the global economy is an environment of conflicting interests and finite opportunities, it is useful to revisit the past and look for evidence of domination and capitulation in trade matters. These are far from original ideas, but themes widely present in the books of popular alternative economists, perhaps presented in a different format with different emphasis.

a) Colonial and Military Dominance—Britannia Rules the Waves

Much like contemporary developing countries, the beginnings of Britain's economic development centred on clothing production. Many may be familiar with the history of technological developments in clothing manufacturing and the factory system that effectively started Britain's industrial revolution. Technology and innovation developments are widely studied and implicitly considered to be the root of Britain's success. Introductory economics students are primarily taught that innovation, and individual hard work and genius, allowed Britain to industrialise first. But the shadowy dimensions of aggressive industrial policy, including tariffs, and later colonial empire trade rules and aggressive trade wars, have had a surprisingly large role in shaping the advantage that Britain eventually gained.

"Henry VII created quite an extensive economic policy toolbox. His first and most important tool was export duties, which ensured that foreign textile producers had to process more expensive raw materials than their English counterparts. Newly established wool manufacturers were also granted tax exemptions for a period, and were given monopolies in certain geographical areas for certain periods. There was also a policy to attract craftsmen and entrepreneurs from abroad, especially from Holland and Italy. As English wool-manufacturing capacity grew, so did the export duties, until England had sufficient production capacity to process all the wool they produced. Then, about a hundred years later, Elizabeth I could place an embargo on all raw wool exports from England.... Florence was one of the states hardest hit by the English competition. The Florentines tried to make do with Spanish wool, and they tried to diversify from wool production to silk, but the English policy was so successful that the golden age of Florence was definitely over.".... "It was the this first wave of globalisation that seriously dug the ditch dividing rich and poor countries in a process in which the colonies, as the practise had been for centuries, were not allowed to industrialise." (Reinert, pp. 80 & 57).

Like Reinert and Chang, it is claimed here that it was not, as many are taught, purely superior ingenuity, enterprise and hard work in manufacturing that gave Britain it's trading dominance. It was instead an effective policy of controlling trade and controlling what economic activities Britain engaged in that sealed the outcome. The British dictated what economic activities they engaged in by an effective brew of colonial control, naval superiority, and aggressive industrial policy including tariffs. They ensured their dominance within the most progressive economic activities, and maintained their country's economic advancement through areas that generated the best positive externalities. Again, the chicken or egg problem has hidden the extent to which positive externalities captured through aggressive industrial policy and export-led growth were in fact the prime mover in causing the technological leaps forward. It was not, as is perhaps commonly misperceived, that the technological leaps forward caused the trade domination.

> "...the policies introduced by Walpole after 1721 were deliberately aimed at promoting manufacturing industries. Introducing the new law, Walpole stated, through the King's address to Parliament: 'it is evident that nothing so much contributes to promote the public well-being as the exportation of manufactured goods and the importation of foreign raw material.' ... Tariffs on imported foreign manufactured goods were significantly raised, while tariffs on raw materials used for manufacture were lowered, or even dropped altogether. Manufacturing exports were encouraged by a series of measures, including export subsidies. Finally, regulation was introduced to control the quality of manufactured products, especially textile products, so that unscrupulous manufacturers could not damage the reputation of British products in foreign markets.

> "These policies are strikingly similar to those used with such success by the 'miracle' economies of East Asia, such as Japan, Korea and Taiwan, after the Second World War. Policies that many believe, as I myself used to, to have been invented by the Japanese policy-makers in the 1950s—such as 'duty drawbacks' on imports for exported manufactured products and the imposition of export product quality standards by the government—were actually early British inventions. Walpole's protectionist policies remained in place for the next century, helping British manufacturing industries to catch up with and then finally forge ahead of their counterparts on the Continent. Britain remained a

highly protectionist country until the mid-19th century. In 1820, Britain's average tariff rate on manufactured imports was 45-55%, compared to 6-8% in the Low Countries, 8-12% in Germany and Switzerland and around 20% in France ... When it came to its colonies, Britain was quite happy to impose an outright ban on advanced manufacturing activities that it did not want developed ... Britain also banned exports from its colonies that competed with its own products, home and abroad....

"Finally, policies were deployed to encourage primary commodity production in the colonies. Walpole provided export subsidies to (on the American side) and abolished import taxes on (on the British side) raw materials produced in the American colonies (such as hemp, wood and timber). He wanted to make absolutely sure that the colonists stuck to producing primary commodities and never emerged as competitors to British manufacturers. Thus they were compelled to leave the most profitable 'high-tech' industries in the hands of Britain—which ensured that Britain would enjoy the benefits of being on the cutting edge of world development." (Chang, p. 44).

Even though cloth manufacturing processes were previously more developed in other places, for example wool in the Low Countries and cotton in India, and despite the fact that cotton was not even grown natively, Britain was able to ensure this trade was captured and retained. Britain's trade remained favourable and profitable, and indeed this was eventually helped by technology and organisational improvements, but initially the advantage was created by using its military and colonial power to restrict and dominate competition.

"....the textile mills of Manchester replaced the weavers of Bengal. In order to illustrate this dramatic effect, Marx quoted the English Governor-General, who wrote home to

> London that, 'The misery hardly finds a parallel in the history of commerce. The bones of the cotton-weavers are bleaching the plains of India." (Reinert, p. 190).

It is well known that the roots of Britain's large empire were in trade, as is illustrated by the fact that its rule over India started out not as the direct rule of one state over another, but as the dominance of sections and interests within certain principalities and trading ports by the East India Company. In the clothing industry, after the initial advantage of dominance paid back its rewards of lucrative trade, the positive externalities of new industries led on to a chain of new scientific discoveries, business practices, applications and products.

> "Adam Smith understood that Walpole's policies were becoming obsolete. Without them, many British industries would have been wiped out before they had the chance to catch up with their superior rivals abroad. But once British industries had become internationally competitive, protection became less necessary and even counter-productive. Protecting industries that do not need protection any more is likely to make them complacent and inefficient, as Smith observed." (Chang, p. 46).

Britain's trading relationships at that time show that it is no coincidence that manufacturing and military power converge first most distinctly in Britain. The Royal Navy is central and a good example of this integration of national interests. In the eighteenth century, Britain was the first country to issue government gilts on a large scale, which was directly motivated by the desire to use this government borrowing to build up its Royal Navy. The national project of the Royal Navy became at that time the biggest economic activity in the country, stimulating economic development by generating positive externalities along the way. Britain had the largest navy in the world right up until WWII. Not only did the early navy require great volumes of unexciting food and wood, but it also stimulated significant positive externalities by generating demand for all the other materials and technologies involved in ship building and running. After all, a warship of that time was the most technologically advanced and expensive 'thing' in the world, loaded with cutting edge technology and innovative improvements, always with the aim of having the edge over other countries. Building and running a warship was an economic activity that boosted economic development and capabilities. Britain's advantage was in recognising that borrowing on a massive scale was worthwhile to achieve the security and dominance of world trade over its European rivals, and it worked.

Business was war, and furthermore war was often sparked by the conflicting of international business interests abroad. The military might of Britain was used to promote national business interests, and the fruits of Britain's successful export trade paid for its military. To control the seas was to control trade, and to control trade was the key to economic success and dominance in positive externality rich economic activities. The tune 'Britannia Rules The Waves' seems a strange irrelevance in our orderly international law abiding world, but in the eighteenth and nineteenth century, nothing was more relevant. Colonies were not allowed to manufacture certain goods. All colonial trade had to flow in British ships – often through British ports – all tariffs and taxes were controlled and collected by Britain, and as late as 1900, it is estimated that half of all world trade flowed through British ports. Along with the other countries that were first to industrialise and develop, they had the inherent advantage themselves of also being first, providing the most scarce and obvious products, unlike today's poor countries that find themselves trying to enter small sections of often peripheral, random and spurious products within mature, competitive and crowded markets.

b) Economic and Cultural Dominance

It is understandable to see how one could come to the conclusion that the United States developed in the textbook free market fashion. The free market ideology would surmise that the US grew by exporting its comparative advantage, which was initially based on its vast farmland and other natural resources. It certainly did have all this, and the ideal capitalist policies and entrepreneurial spirit to succeed, which makes it unsurprising that many individuals and organisations based in the United States continue to presume that this should work for others. However, to believe only this is, like the British example, missing out an entire overlooked vein of the history of industrial policy within the United States which, for a country now preaching free trade and lower tariffs, is surprising to learn about. Both Reinert and Chang attribute a great deal of early US economic success to the policies first championed by one of the first major figures in American politics, Alexander Hamilton, the country's first finance minister (treasury secretary).

> "In 1791, Hamilton submitted his Report on the Subject of Manufactures to the US Congress. In it, he expounded his view that the country needed a big programme to develop its industries. The core of his idea was that a backward country like the US should protect its 'industries in their infancy' from foreign competition and nurture them to the point where they could stand on their own feet. ... Although Hamilton rightly cautioned against taking these policies too far, they are, nevertheless, a pretty potent and 'heretical' set of policy prescriptions. Were he finance minister of a developing country today, the IMF and the World Bank would certainly have refused to lend money to his country and would be lobbying for his removal from office ... Although Hamilton's trade policy was well established by the 1820's, tariffs were an ever-present source of tension in

US politics for the following three decades. The Southern agrarian states constantly attempted to lower industrial tariffs, while the Northern manufacturing states argued the case for keeping them high or even raising them ...

"Many Americans call Abraham Lincoln, the 16th president (1861-65), the Great Emancipator—of the American slaves. But he might equally be labelled the Great Protector—of American manufacturing. Lincoln was a strong advocate of infant industry protection. He cut his political teeth under Henry Clay of the Whig Party, who advocated the building of the 'American System,' which consisted of infant industry protection ('Protection for Home Industries,' in Clay's words) and investment in infrastructure such as canals ('Internal Improvements'). ... Historians of the period agree that his [Lincoln's] abolition of slavery in 1862 was more of a strategic move to win the war than an act of moral conviction. Disagreement over trade policy, in fact was at least as important as, and possibly more important than, slavery in bringing about the Civil War. ... once elected, Lincoln raised industrial tariffs to their highest level so far in US history. The expenditure for the Civil War was given as an excuse ... However, after the war, tariffs stayed at wartime levels or above. Tariffs on manufactured imports remained at 40-50% until the First World War, and were the highest of any country in the world. (Chang, pp. 49–54).

Reinert also agrees that evidence of this alternative flavour of American economic history can be implicated in the Civil War, when the two sides had diametrically opposed intensions in terms of how much industrial policy the country as a whole should pursue. The Northern progressive states wanted an active industrial policy to restrict trade with the contemporary dominant overseas manufactures of that time, mainly Britain, in favour of supporting and developing their own emerging industrial potential. The more traditional Southern states, on the other hand, wanted a continuation of free trade, in order to favour their own agricultural produce. The South would thrive under free trade conditions because it was selling these agricultural goods to European manufacturing countries that was clearly America's comparative advantage at that time. In line with its own economic self-interest, Britain predictably supported the Southern states. The North won partly through the merit of its industrial advantage, and the United States continued to follow a surprisingly active and potent industrial policy right up until it became the leading industrial producer of the world.

> "In nineteenth-century America, Irish immigrant workers were keenly supporting the 'American System of Manufactures,' the protective system that allowed the country to industrialise. They remembered that Ireland had had her industry stolen from her, and did not want their new country to be subject to the same treatment by England (who vehemently protested against American industrialisation for more than a hundred years)."... "In spite of its natural protection through high transportation costs, the United States chose to build its enormous steel industry behind tariff walls of up to 100 per cent." (Reinert, pp. 99 & 58).

Later, the United States benefited profoundly from the effects of the two world wars in Europe, both in the lead that they gained as a result of the harm done to Europe's output and wealth, and the benefit of the extra demand for resources that the war created and America supplied.

> "Only after Britain had sold off the family silver to pay for the nozzle would America 'lend' Britain its garden hose to fight the Hitlerian fire. ... while we were gearing up to come to the rescue, we squeezed the British. ... When

World War II was over, the United States, not Britain, had all the money." (Cohen & DeLong, p. 18).

Previously, Europe was the investor in the new world, which included the United States, but by now Europe had liquidated or destroyed its capital assets and the United States had become the most capital-rich major country in the world. America grew to become the superior trader of consumer and technology goods and brands, and outgrew its European competitors. The US domination was helped by the prominence of the dollar conquering the British pound as the world's default currency of choice. This dominance of the dollar in world trade, the advantage of the large home consumer market, and the successful brands and lifestyle that it portrayed, all served to boost US export domination and the success of US companies establishing themselves abroad. The entrepreneur business values and trading mentality has and continues to benefit the US greatly, but its cultural and economic dominance exaggerate the benefits that it receives from these qualities.

> "Industry, and gradually also the workers, were protected by huge market power, could keep the prices up, and avoid 'perfect competition.' Industrialism has gelled as John Kenneth Galbraith's 'balance of countervailing powers,' that is, as a system where wealth was based on extremely imperfect competition both in the labour market and in the market for products. Industrialism was a system based on a triple rent-seeking by capitalists, workers and the state. The perfect competition of textbook economics was found only in the Third World." (Reinert, p. 134).

For the last 80 years, the American cultural dominance in areas such as films and television has helped to promote and introduce brands from its companies to the wider world, retaining its profitable position. The companies of the United States have also built on this advantage by further succeeding to dominate many aspects of business through intellectual copyright laws and franchising, as well as by straightforward ownership of resources through foreign direct investment.

> "Because America had the money—had it solidly, rightfully, self-assuredly, and durably—for about one hundred years, people all over the world wanted to be like Americans ... Soft power—not military might, not straight-out money, but the ability to inspire acceptance and imitation—was a vital component of American international dominance." (Cohen & DeLong, p.57).

> "Moreover, even when it shifted to a freer (if not absolutely free) trade, the US government promoted key industries by another means, namely, public funding of R&D. Between the 1950s and the mid-1990s, US federal government funding accounted for 50-70% of the country's total R&D funding, which is way above the figures, around 20%, found in such 'government-led' countries as Japan and Korea. Without federal government funding for R&D, the US would not have been able to maintain its technological lead over the rest of the world in key industries like computers, semiconductors, life sciences, the internet and aerospace." (Chang, p. 55-56).

Although the United States could be said to remain on top due to free trade and liberal market values, it got on top thanks to a big dollop of industrial policy, most notably severe protectionism early on and state supported military spending and R& D more recently. If the South had won the Civil War and comparative advantage and free trade had prevailed, perhaps the United States would now be a less-industrialised country, more like Argentina or Brazil.

> "Countries [that were] already wealthy could afford a very different policy from those of countries still poor. In fact,

once a country had been solidly industrialised, the very same factors that required initial protection—achieving increasing returns and acquiring new technologies—now required bigger and more international markets in order to develop and prosper. Successful industrial protection thus carries the seeds of its own destruction: when successful, the protection that was initially required becomes counter productive." (Reinert, p. 81).

"In brief, the American view as expressed in its domestic politics, in its positions in international forums, and in the discourse of its economists is that industrial policy is largely a form of cheating. At best it unfairly free-rides on the overall system, and usually it backfires and ensnares the intervening government into taxing the healthy parts of its economy to support losers. We don't do it. Proper Europeans older than fifty will eagerly tell you that this insistently proclaimed American view is disingenuous. Americans didn't call it industrial policy; they called it defence." ... "Even the United States, under the politically protective aegis of defence, spun off fully fledged, advanced industries such as commercial jets and computers—industries that quickly soared to global dominance. What part of US leadership in the advanced sectors would exist in its current form without the Defence Advanced Research Projects Agency (DARPA), the National Institute of Health (NIH), and US research universities? Jet aircraft in Seattle and biotech and electronics around Boston and California's Silicon Valley were always inconceivable without the Massachusetts Institute of Technology, without Stanford, without NIH, and without the Pentagon." ... "With peace time defence spending levels passing 9 percent of GDP, much of that invested in and producing what were for the time the highest of high-tech products." ... "There were always two profound exceptions to the logic of neo-liberalism. The first is spending on national defence, including science and technology to support defence where the United States spends more than the next fifteen countries combined." (Cohen & DeLong, pp. 135, 10-11, 42 & 53).

c) The Cold War Benefactors

> "... the goal of the Marshall Plan was not only to reindustrialise Germany, but also to establish a *cordon sanitaire* of wealthy nations along the borders of the Communist Bloc in Europe and Asia ..." ... "When it was important to build a defence line to protect Asia and Europe from communist threat, the United States understood that the way to create wealth was to industrialise the nations bordering communism ... Once the communist threat had dissolved, the developed countries rapidly started applying ... a type of economic policy that resembled old British colonial policy at its worst." (Reinert, pp. 241 & 211).

In the post-war decades, Japan, and later the four Asian Tigers, South Korea, Taiwan, Hong Kong, and Singapore, benefited greatly from favourable trade. The trading relationships these countries had were heavily affected by the Cold War objectives of the United States and other Western nations. Throughout the Cold War, trade policy and aid, such as the initial Marshall plan, were influenced and motivated by the fear of the spread of communism. Many wise and unwise projects, undesirable regimes and immoral arms deals were supported or tolerated during the period, due to the wider objectives of the Cold War on both sides. Undoubtedly, the technical and economic achievements of Japan and these Asian Tiger countries cannot be belittled. The masterly role of their respective state officials in using industrial policy and periods of import substitution effectively to generate positive externalities and industrial capacity was impressive. However, even with these commendations duly paid to the countries concerned, the aggressive export-led mercantilist trade policies that helped to grow these countries were largely dependant on a willing United States and Western Europe which readily tolerated the often detrimental trading relationships.

Japan, for example, was given positive media coverage after the war by the US government to heal over the bitter aftertaste remaining from the Pacific war, encouraging Americans to have closer trade and business links with Japan. During the Cold War, both sides used economic measures, both positive and negative, for political goals, and many countries were affected, but it was the countries mentioned above that can be thought of as the clearest benefactors in terms of the comprehensive accession into economic development. Ultimately, their aggressive non-reciprocal export-led trade relationships with the West were largely tolerated because of the Cold War.

> "America felt itself to be so unchallengeably rich and powerful that it permitted the Japanese to hold down the value of the yen for a generation and rebuild their economy on the basis of exports of industrial products into the United States—even at the eventual expense of American industries such as steel, shipbuilding, automobiles, and machine tools. This was a bearable cost of Cold War-era global leadership." (Cohen & DeLong, p. 19-20).

The scarce examples of success provided by these countries have been vehemently fought over by different economic schools of thought. But it could be concluded that the more you look, the less their example can be used as a validation of globalisation and free market policies

> "Singapore has had free trade and relied heavily on foreign investment, but, even so, it does not conform in other respects to the neo-liberal ideal. Though it welcomed

foreign investors, it used considerable subsidies in order to attract transnational corporations in industries it considered strategic, especially in the form of government investment in infrastructure and education targeted at particular industries. Moreover it has one of the largest state-owned enterprise sectors in the world, including the Housing Development Board, which supplies 85% of all housing (almost all land is owned by the government)." ... "It is a sleight of hand that free trade economists have so effectively deployed in cowing their opponents—if you are against free trade, they insinuate, you must be against progress. As South Korea shows, active participation in international trade does not require free trade. Indeed, had South Korea pursued free trade and not promoted infant industries, it would not have become a major trading nation. It would still be exporting raw materials (e.g., tungsten ore, fish, seaweed) or low-technology, low-price products (e.g., textiles, garments, wigs made with human hair)..." (Chang, pp 29 & 82).

d) The Control Economy Giant

"The foreign-dominated export sector served China not only as a job and income creator, but also as a kind of craft school, and while education is expensive, it is usually worthwhile. ... Most economic growth does not come from adding to visible productive resources—the number of hands and machines, and the skills that formal education has given those hands—but from working smarter. If you sell the results of your workers' hands and your machines for less than they cost, but in the process acquire the knowledge needed to work smarter, you come out ahead. And imitation and practise are the best ways to do so. An enormous share of China's economic growth is an unrecompensed by-product of what businesses do as technological and organisational knowledge that spills over into the local industrial ecosystem." (Cohen & Delong, p. 97).

To summarise the vast subject of China's development successes, it first could be said that China has managed to undercut and dominate the world's production of medium technology manufactured goods. These goods are exactly the types that generate the positive externalities central to an 'activities matter' explanation of economic development. The measured way in which it has grafted market policies and export production onto and into a formally communist and centrally controlled economy has been very single-minded, pragmatic and effective. One of the most notable aspects of China' development has been the deliberate allocation of special zones of economic development along its coast. These zones have been designed to attract and facilitate export-oriented business activity, as discussed in chapter one. Remember the analogy of the burning coal fire and critical mass representing maximum positive externalities. This regional separation and specialisation has partly been necessitated by China's conflicting desire to be both a leading participator in the world capitalist economy, and a functioning massive centrally-governed state containing millions of poor, agricultural peasants. The use of zones also reflects China's experimental approach to development, caused partly by its unique situation, and partly by its resistance to the wholesale adoption and trust in Western capitalist ideology regarding what developing countries should do. China is inoculated from swallowing free trade mythology due to its historical experiences at the hands of Western powers.

> "Somewhat later, while the US and Europe were still protecting their industries, China and Japan were forced, with the help of military threats and power, to sign treaties where they agreed *not* to protect theirs. For a while, China and Japan became, economically, virtual colonies.

In Japanese and Chinese history books, these unfair treaties retain importance and are still regarded with indignation." (Reinert, p. 60).

As discussed earlier, China's economic zones have been generally effective by concentrating and focusing the positive externalities that trading businesses of this kind both require from and emit into specific local regions. Part of the understanding of China's success can be found in comparing and contrasting it and its actions with those of other developing countries. The Chinese economy, through its large size and high level of state control and restrictions, has been able to withstand many of the negative ongoing effects and the occasional turbulent storms that have affected the smaller, more open economies. However, China's more mercantilist growth strategy has, like the example of the Cold War benefactors above, relied on the industrialised world absorbing some of its negative implications. China has used currency exchange controls and import restrictions to limit the amount of reciprocal trade that it undertakes with rich countries. Chinese wages are still low, even after roughly two decades of strong growth, especially compared with rich countries when they were at the same stage of development. This is perpetuated both by the large reservoir of the poor rural population competing for jobs, and by the state-controlled nature of the economy indicated above.

The advantages that China gains from this are compounded by the consumer preferences of the Chinese population, which at present, thanks to its own feelings and experiences of uncertainty has a strong desire to save. Furthermore, the Chinese people have had a relatively low propensity to spend their acquired hard currency on consumer goods from Western countries for cultural reasons. However, this will change as the population becomes richer and feels more secure. But in the meantime, the uneven trading relationship that China has with the rest of the world requires what is referred to here as 'capitulation' by its trading partners. China has taken the option of recirculating its dollars, euros and pounds back to the Western countries in the form of capital and loans – which is controversial in itself, and presently a major factor in current international economics.[4]

The impact of this large new presence in the world economy has been viewed as causing significant implications and distortions in other countries. In the decade before the recession, inflation in the West was kept low by cheap Chinese goods and the cheap credit available originating from Chinese savings. A simplistic interpretation could be that the Chinese lent us their export earnings, which helped us to buy even more of their exports. However, as this book is being

---

[4] Note to non-economists: the imbalance of capital flows is an inevitable result and mirror image of an imbalance of trade flows as dictated by basic economic laws of trade. The dollars, euros or pounds paid for imports have to come back somehow to their home countries to be of any value to the exporting country and to pay their production costs. If this money does not return in the form of purchasing physical goods or services in the opposite direction (for example, China buying Western countries' exports), then it must return in the form of purchasing capital assets in the importing country or as loans made to the importer countries in the importer's currency.

The law dictates that the degree to which China does not reciprocate imports of physical goods with rich countries will, through the mechanisms of money flows, match the degree to which the surplus dollars, euros and pounds they have earned will find their way into being used to buy rich country assets or support rich country borrowing. A country that is not reciprocating physical trade, like Saudi Arabia with its oil revenues, or China with its trade imbalance, will therefore be a country that lends its unspent foreign hard currency or buys up assets in the importing countries. This explains why Saudis own many expensive properties in London, and why China holds a substantial proportion of US government debt.

written, the debt-financed consumer boom and asset bubble nurtured during this decadent era has reached its bloated peak and burst. This demonstrates that China's huge size, productive potential, and deliberate trade imbalance will continue to have significant effects on the world economy. The trade relationships of China and the West will be central to the narrative explaining the biggest economic changes in the near future.

Over the last few decades, the right-wing Washington consensus organisations and economists on one hand, and the more left-wing sympathetic charitable NGOs on the other hand, have both been striving to reduce world poverty through following and propagating their own contrasting, sometimes dogmatic views. In the meantime, the unlikely mix of policies and actions of the firstly unelected and furthermore nominally communist bureaucrats of China have, through economic trade, arguably done more for poverty reduction in the world than both of the former groups put together.

e) The English-Speaking Office

India is the second giant of third world development success. Although it is still a country with very high inequality, it contains many vibrant world class centres of trade and industry. In the past, India's attitude to economics and trade was understandably shaped by its experience of the de-industrialising nature of British colonial rule. Britain's imperial control of India's trade forced it to reduce or crystallise its industrial capability and instead become a supplier of raw materials. Unlike most other colonised countries, India had an existing world-class export industry in textiles before it was colonised, and the national cultural memory of watching this trade be apprehended by the British has probably inoculated it against the temptations of free market rhetoric. Subsequently, some observers would argue, India in its first decades of independence went too far in the direction of a planned economy and industrial policy implementation, perhaps as a reaction to its history.

> "...even after the early 1990s trade liberalisation, India's average manufacturing tariffs remained at above 30% (it is still 25% today) ... India has also imposed severe restrictions on foreign direct investment—entry restrictions, ownership restrictions and various performance requirements (e.g., local contents requirements)." (Chang, p. 30).

Recently, like China, India has moved its economic outlook a step closer to free trade, but has been careful to nurture and expand key clusters of activity. Firstly by harnessing the well-educated English-speaking segment of its population, India has developed a cluster of activities around outsourcing the back room services, call centres and IT skills. India has become a world leader in the area of computer programming and other IT-related creative activities. India's cheaper, high calibre graduate personnel can win contracts from higher cost rich country businesses. Besides these two flagship areas, India has steadily developed as a manufacturing centre and also an important centre for agricultural and bio research.

India has been a heavy user of planning and has generated many concentrated centres of speciality, such as Mumbai and Bangalore. These cluster locations fit with the positive externality and industrial policy themes discussed. India's model of development is closer to the free market norm than the more centrally planned and unique China, but India still provides an example of a country with a history of free market *unfriendly* policies and heavy state interference succeeding in economic development. This is in contrast to other countries that have been swallowing the free market medicine more obediently and who have not done as well.

Significantly for the concept of the reservoir of poor country labour detailed later, India, like China, still has a large reservoir of rural population yet to draw into its more productive sectors.

Instances of Domination and Capitulation: From Hard Power Through to Ideology

The five examples of winning above could all be said to all contain evidence of domination and/or capitulation in trade matters. Britain, when it was the workshop of the world, forced and encouraged its colonies and other countries to specialise in agricultural goods and commodities. There was global trade, but it was not 'free' – it was controlled by Britain and others, who understood their own manufacturing interests very keenly. Britain policed and protected these interests through that most massive national financial and economic commitment, the Royal Navy. There was no concept at that time of docilely accepting your comparative advantage, or of free trade harmony between the ambitious European powers. Britain decided what sectors it wanted to dominate, decided where in the world it could sell to, banned competition in these countries if it could, and fought trade wars in other instances. Furthermore, Britain attempted to control all the major ocean trade routes and attempted to make sure as much as possible, that trade took place on British ships through British ports. These facts show a country geared towards dominating an environment full of conflicting and competing interests, rather than the patient, docile harmony suggested by the free trade ideology.

> "In the seventeenth and eighteenth centuries, the British East India Company had the mother of all strategic positions. The company made today's Microsoft look like a timid mom-and-pop shop by comparison. It completely monopolised trade in four countries, had

worldwide interests ranging from coffee and woollens to opium, had its own private army and navy, and was empowered by the crown to declare war in circumstances when its business interests were threatened, and effectively ruled over a fifth of the world's population." (Beinhocker, p. 329).

When Britain became industrialised, it quickly became a net importer of food, and the repeal of the Corn Laws can be interpreted as an integral part of British industrial policy, reinforcing Britain's role as an exporter of manufactured goods. It further reinforced other countries' role as agricultural and commodity suppliers to the more developed Britain. Britain had previously also enacted Empire Trade laws which forbade its colonies from entering certain manufacturing sectors. Britain's domination was not only through superior production ability, but it was preordained and designed by military and political power.

The United States in its most impressive growth period used tariffs heavily to nurture its industry. Then, when it reached and overtook Europe, it became the great innovator and brand leader, only giving up old technology enterprises to competitors abroad. In its most dominant period, the United States exported high value-added goods, and imported cheaper labour-intensive goods where fewer positive externalities and future innovation were likely to be found. In terms of domination, one of the most controversial areas of US history is in its dealings and political interferences in less developed countries during the Cold War. At face value, much of what the US did could be thought of as purely driven by anti-communist and anti-Soviet motives. But under this broad umbrella, many controversial actions have the side effect of not only fighting communism, but also supporting US business interests abroad. There is a grey area and a difficult line to be drawn between fighting anti-capitalists in less developed countries, and using your military and intelligence resources to aid your own country's capitalist business interests.[5]

Emphasising the importance of different economic activities also supports a left-wing interpretation of many political struggles. Join together these ideas with the history of the capitalist US supporting its free market friends in other countries, and suddenly issues can become more controversial. If, as asserted earlier, the interests of a developing country as a whole are to move away from free trade, but the interests of the rich country are to keep it there, certain events in history can seem more controversial. This points to a left-wing radical analysis as follows: assume a poor country is run by elites, assume the main route to becoming an elite in a poor country is gaining wealth through the production of agricultural goods and commodities, and assume that elites will defend their own economic security and therefore these sectors, even at cost to the wider interests of the whole country.

The conclusion would be that, given the different contributions different economic activities can make to development, the

---

[5] For a more cynical analysis of US methods of achieving domination or capitulation within the arena of world trade relationships, read John Perkins's *Confessions of an Economic Hit Man*. Perkins details the actions of the governments and intelligence agencies of the United States and the West in interfering in other countries. These actions were under the guise of being for Cold War or development objectives, but he argues often they were actually motivated by the unscrupulous economic interests of influential large corporations, secret government objectives or trade interests in general. It could be argued that the contrast is highlighted by his book between the out right military invasion and subjugation as happened throughout mankind's more xenophobic and nationalistic history, and the more clandestine and concealed dirty work that has to be resorted to in our more modern fair minded and liberal culture, where the general public may benefit from economic domination, but would never sanction certain means of achieving it.

elites are making the country capitulate to an unfavourable trade relationship and subverting the common good. This analysis becomes more potent if an outside interest is supporting the elites, for example the capitalists interests of the US supporting the commodity and agricultural producing elites in South America. The capitalist interests of the US would wish to maintain South America within this role of a commodity and agricultural producer, and not wish it to industrialise by using tariffs and other industrial policy. This is comparable to when Britain supported the free trade Southern Confederacy against the pro-industry, pro-industrial policy Yankees in the US civil war.

There are many examples of actors in a political circumstance rigidly following their personal interest. Wealthy land owners in many situations would be quite happy to continue to maintain their own relative personal power, wealth and influence, and import manufactured goods instead of attempting to make them. They would rather be the richest within a poor country than competing with the emerging industrialists in a developing country. This could describe the Tory landowner MPs who supported the Corn Laws in Britain that held back manufacturing, or the southern plantation owners in the American Civil War, or the landowning elites in some South American countries. The actions of countries can be dictated by the individual elites' self-interests and not the general long-term interests of the country's whole population. Reinert notes the following as one explanation for the prosperity of 15th century Florence.

> "In Florence, the most important European city-state not situated on the coast, the big landowners had been for centuries kept from having any political power. Consequently, as in the coastal states, the interests of craftsmen, manufacturers and traders dominated the life of the city ... This historically crucial link between political structure

and economic structure—between democracy and an economy diversified away from dependence on agriculture and raw materials—is another crucial historical lesson lost today..." (Reinert, p. 77-78).

Empires, gunboat trade diplomacy, and excessive interference in poor countries' political affairs have thankfully become more scrutinised and socially unacceptable in modern democratic countries. There was a time when the population of rich countries celebrated the conquest and subjugation of others, but thankfully now people are more moral, empathetic and conscientious regarding foreigners, as decent over recent conflicts show. It could be argued that with military and political force no longer available to rich countries' business interests, the power of ideology itself has become the tool to encourage poorer countries to capitulate their trade interests. The free market ideology could be interpreted as a post-colonial or post-gunboat method of resolving or avoiding the clash of trade interests discussed above. With absolute force no longer acceptable, the rich countries can seek to maintain the status quo by promoting a doctrine that attempts to convince poor and developing countries that their best interest is in maintaining their present comparative advantage. Rather than forcing poor countries to remain unindustrialised through empires, treaties and trading enclaves backed up by gunboats, the modern hegemony harnesses the power of free market ideology through pervasive international institutions. It could be argued that the trade interests of the rich countries are now kept by the WTO, backed up by the World Bank and IMF, instead of the British Royal Navy docking in Bombay and Shanghai, and instead of the CIA interfering in South American politics by supporting conservative agricultural elites against socialist progressives.

> "Before David Ricardo there was little doubt that emulation would be the best strategy, and historically the

most important contribution of Ricardo's trade theory was that, for the first time, it made colonialism morally defensible." (Reinert, p. xxiii).

Reinert can make this claim because Ricardo's theory of comparative advantage, applied mathematically, would advise that poor countries should continue to specialise in supplying commodities and agricultural goods to their colonial masters. This is in contrast to economists earlier in history who would have advised attempting to emulate and industrialise. Supplying agricultural goods or commodities would be their *present* optimum behaviour, according to Ricardo, and all thoughts of the future or development were not a factor in Ricardo's theory. Just as Ricardo's comparative advantage could be argued to have made colonialism more acceptable, the free market policies genuinely believed by many economists and leaders, has made neo-colonial type domination of rich countries over poor countries in recent decades appear less self-interested or immoral.

The exceptional position in time and location of the Cold War benefactor countries mentioned in the last section meant that they were fortunate enough to experience the trade capitulation of a tolerant US and Western world. In this case, the US and other Western countries choose to capitulate by absorbing the Cold War benefactors' exports resulting from their strongly mercantilist policies. These countries – Japan, South Korea, Singapore, Taiwan and British Hong Kong – were required to be shining examples of the superiority of free market capitalism over communism. For critics of the free market ideology, it is revealing that when the US and the West really *had* to achieve instances of economic development to counter the cold war threats, they were able to ignore purist free market doctrine and instead recall the export led growth methods from their own earlier histories. South Korea and Japan were given favourable unreciprocated trade relationships by the US and the rest of the

West, which allowed them to become impressive examples of the merits of capitalism on China's and Russia's doorstep. At the same time other less strategic countries were not, and as the previous chapter seeks to demonstrate, *could not all* be granted the same capitulation of Western trade interests.

Presently the free market ideology has provided what could be a capitulation of unprecedented historical proportions, towards China, a country that does not believe in western capitalism anyway. The adherence to free market principles has encouraged rich countries to tolerate and capitulate to the aggressive export led trade practises of China. China has not been granted this privilege like the cold war benefactors above, but has just taken it through being the biggest and the most deliberate player of the export-led growth game. China has been able to succeed in its own example of economic capitulation at the expense of its richer and greedier fellow countries. The West has so far tolerated or capitulated towards accepting China's exports without reciprocal imports, partly because its free trade and comparative advantage ideology blinds believers to the damage this could do, and partly because it is instead willing to live beyond its means in a state of decadence. The imbalance of China's economic trading activity has coincided with, and indeed germinated, the recent decadent credit binge and asset bubble of the Western world. The West was happy to use China's cheap exports and savings to prolong low interest rates (their lending) and low inflation (their cheaper goods) to sustain the massive debt fuelled binge and asset bubble. In this decadent fashion, the West was instead willing to tolerate China buying its assets and tolerate the Western populations and now governments racking up vast amounts of credit owed to China instead.

When applying the analysis put forward earlier, this can be perceived as an example of capitulation, where wealthy Western societies may prioritise cheap goods and extra consumption over the loss of their economic advantage in the long term. Unlike examples from history, the rich countries of the world have given up the production of positive externality producing goods without any non-economic power advantage from China. The developed countries have 'let in' the goods from China's one-sided export strategy, not because China dominates them, but they have capitulated by their own free will for ideological as well as decadent reasons. The cheap goods from China have made them temporarily richer, but this capitulation may have lost them some of their economic power and advantage. In the West, the hangover from this decadent binge generated by China's asymmetrical trade relationship is now highlighting the rich countries' compromised actual ability to earn money on the world trade stage. When the rich countries try to recover from a boom built on an empty bubble, it will highlight the extent of the trade they have lost to China and others. This type of capitulation could be described as a positive contribution to world economic development, even though it may be detrimental to the decadent rich countries involved. Millions of Chinese are being lifted out of poverty; therefore, it may be in the greater world's interest for the developed countries to capitulate. But if the rich countries of the world remain in economic trouble, there is little reason to think they will lead the way in sorting out other international problems.

> "Wedded as it [the US] is to the Ricardian view that one-way free trade is fine, it feels that we shouldn't get too upset if other countries want to sell and not buy. If they want to manage currency values to keep their imports cheap or subsidise their exports and dump in our markets, it's a kind of gift to our consumers." (Prestowitz, p. 250).

The Losers: Specialising in Being Poor

Much of the remit of this book and much of the contemporary discussion within development economics is to address and explain failure. Many poor countries are further away than ever from achieving any substantial development success, despite the supposedly more 'free' geopolitical environment. The present inequality and poverty of this world is a shocking failure, especially considering the knowledge and progress humans have made in other fields, and considering the hopes and expectations of earlier times. Previous drafts of this book devoted a much larger section to this topic. However the conclusion has been arrived at that this subject has been already covered comprehensively by superior authors such as Reinert, Chang, Collier and De Rivero. As a result, a more brief discussion is sought here, focusing on the positive externality and economic activities matter themes.

For example Reinert below discusses the manufacture of two seemingly similar products with contrasting production dynamics, baseballs and golf balls. Golf balls can be manufactured by machine, but baseballs have to be sewn by hand. Considering the wages of the American factory workers with the South American stitchers, rough export n time which makes certain trade relationships so uneven. will succeed over the sellers wish to achieve higher pReinert notes:

> "The poverty of Haiti and the wealth of the United States are, for both countries, simultaneously a cause of and a result of the choice of what to produce. The institution we call 'the market' rewards the world's most efficient producer of golf balls with an income between 12 and 36 times—from $0.30–$1 versus $14–$16 per hour—more than the world's most effective producer of baseballs.... Once a considerable gap in real wages has been created, the world market will automatically assign economic activities that are technological dead ends—and therefore only require unqualified labour, for example, to produce baseballs—to low wage countries....The magic of the market will tend to enlarge already existing asymmetries

between rich and poor countries." ... "When ... free trade suddenly opens up between a relatively advanced and a relatively backward nation, the most advanced and knowledge-intensive industry in the least advanced country will tend to die out."[6] ...

"Today, the outsourcing of unmechanisable products from the United States to Mexico and other neighbouring countries recreates the conditions of the nineteenth-century home-workers of Europe ... A similar *maquila* effect is found in agriculture: the mechanisable production (harvesting wheat and maize) is taken over by the United States, while Mexico specialises in the unmechanisable production (harvesting strawberries, citrus fruit, cucumbers and tomatoes), which reduces Mexico's opportunities for innovation, locking the country into technological dead ends and/or activities that retain labour-intensive processes." (Reinert, pp. 113 & 181 & 111).

As this chapter and the last chapter have proposed, there is a conflict of interest at the heart of international trade relations, and the losers have lost this battle for different reasons over the decades. Basically, the source of economic progress is proposed to derive from positive externalities, which flow only from certain economic activities. The loser countries have not been able to become involved in these economic activities for different reasons. There are a vast number of other issues and arguments in this subject of development economics, but it could be argued that this is the key one. There has been an ongoing race happening in global development. In this race the poor countries have started late by being too backward at first, and then they were often subjugated economically under colonialism, and more recently have been kept in their place by a divisive free market ideology. The recent pressures placed

---

[6] This tendency Reinert refers to as the Vanek-Reinert effect.

upon them through the ideological influences of the Washington institutions has crystallised them in their present state of underdevelopment by encouraging them to follow what they already do, rather than having an ambition to move into other activities.

> "The spread of wealth in Europe, and later in the other developed parts of the world, was a result of conscious policies of emulation: the market was a force tamed, like the wind, for the purpose of reaching a defined goal or destination. You may not necessarily be going in the direction that the wind, or the market, happens to be blowing. Cumulative factors and path dependencies cause the winds of the market to blow towards progress only when a high level of development has already been reached. The poorer the nation, the less the winds of laissez-faire blow in the right direction. For this reason, the issue of free trade and other policy decisions is one of context and timing." (Reinert, p. 18).

"In relation to the developing countries, the neo-liberal agenda has been pushed by an alliance of rich country governments led by the US and mediated by the 'Unholy Trinity' of international economic organisations that they largely control—the International Monetary Fund (IMF), The World Bank and the World Trade Organisation (WTO). The rich governments use their aid budgets and access to their home markets as carrots to induce the developing countries to adopt neo-liberal policies. This is sometimes to benefit specific firms that lobby, but usually to create an environment in the developing country concerned that is friendly to foreign goods and investment in general. The IMF and the World Bank play their part by attaching to their loans the condition that recipient countries adopt neo-liberal policies. The WTO contributes by making trading rules that favour free trade in areas where the rich countries are stronger but not where they are weak (e.g., agriculture or textiles)." (Chang, p. 13).

"If IMF agreements are sometimes counterproductive, why do governments enter into such agreements? Usually it is because the government is myopic—a financial crisis makes it desperate for a loan right away, no matter what the long-term consequences. The IMF is often the only way to get such a loan." ... "The world needs some kind of an international financial crisis manager like the IMF. But the IMF fudged its mission beyond short-term crisis bailouts to be a repeat lender to deadbeat governments, with the idea that it was promoting 'structural adjustment' ... No amount of rhetoric can paper over the contradiction between the IMF dictating conditions and 'popular participation.' We will tell you what to do, as well as promise you that you are doing it of your own free will." (Easterly, pp. 189 & 206).

"Will globalisation improve the situation? We have been through what it is likely to do for the countries at the bottom. Trade is more likely to lock them into natural resource dependence than to open new opportunities, and the international mobility of capital and skilled workers is more likely to bleed them of their scant capital and talent than to provide an engine of growth." (Collier, p. 175).

Of most relevance to the positive externalities approach used here, the poor countries treated by the IMF were persuaded to stop supporting any manufacturing enterprises that could not compete with the world's biggest and best producers. The poor countries were encouraged or strong-armed into dropping any subsidies or tariffs that enabled these industries to survive against larger international competitors. Instead, the poor countries were urged to focus on what produce they could sell in open world markets competitively with no state support.

These free market theories led countries to follow their comparative advantage and therefore they primarily ended up increasing their production within agricultural products, other commodities and the most basic manufactured products that relied on cheap labour. These policies and changes have worked to a degree for some developing countries, but not without sacrifice, and for many others, this approach has not worked at all.

Behind the mission towards this free market ideal were the theoretical justifications for the ideology. A belief that a chain of causations and relationships would take place that would increase the country's fortunes in the long-run, formed the foundations for these theories. This belief mainly rested on the assumptions and theories of comparative advantage and the benefits of free trade, and can be explained roughly as follows: opening up poor countries to international trade would increase possible markets, which would then encourage specialisation, investment and the improved use of technology and innovation. This would then create greater efficiency, which would increase wealth, which could be spent or reinvested and would spark further demand and increased productive capacity, which would cause further trade. The goods and services produced and consumed as a whole, would be produced on larger scales in the most efficient way possible in the best, most suitable location, and everyone would subsequently benefit from this larger cake of economic activity.

If successful, this would be a self-feeding positive cycle of growing trade and wealth. In this cycle, the net gains from the efficiencies of free trade causes increased wealth that feeds back into the world economy to benefit everyone. Every business and every country should specialise in what it does best, which will generate more trade and wealth. These were the theories, but great things did not happen.

"The brutal truth is that, however liberal the regulatory regime, foreign firms won't come into a country unless its economy offers an attractive market and high-quality productive resources (labour, infrastructure). This is why so many developing countries have failed to attract significant amounts of FDI, despite giving foreign firms maximum degrees of freedom. Countries have to get growth going *before* TNCs [trans-national corporations] get interested in them. If you are organising a party, it is not enough to tell people that they can come and do whatever they want. People go to parties where they know there are already interesting things happening." (Chang, p. 99).

Even Collier, who once worked for the World Bank and who can be generally thought of as broadly in favour of the free market ideology, reveals with hindsight the excessive free market dogma present in the 1990s, considered now a high water time for this kind of thinking.

"Aid should have been financing the regional transport corridors that are the lifelines for the landlocked. It has largely failed to do so. Why? One reason was that in the 1990s, infrastructure went out of fashion, at least for aid agencies. This was partly because there was an exaggerated belief that the private sector would finance infrastructure, so the aid agencies had better find something else to justify their continued existence. For example, in the World Bank, an agency whose core business had been infrastructure, infrastructure was now lumped in with private sector development and finance, the whole package being merely one of five 'networks'." (Collier, p. 107-108).

This illustrates the extreme to which the free market ideology dominated development economics in the confident years after the fall of communism. Even the classic free rider and common good theories contained in introductory economics courses and central to questions of infrastructure and state provision, were overpowered by the new belief that the private sector will provide all. Given the central role infrastructure plays as a positive externality in development, it is obvious how this ideology can be described here as harming development.

When considered alongside the themes of the previous chapters, the reason why the free market model failed to help poor countries develop is apparent. Although the trade liberalisation policies may have increased specialisation, efficiency and productive capacity in many instances, the benefits of these changes were spread unevenly towards the wealthier countries. The rich countries had their terms of trade improved, but did not increase their demand for goods from the poor countries to the same proportion. Demand may have risen steadily for poor country exports, but not enough to match the extent to which poor countries had reduced their prices and increased potential supply. The areas of production into which the poor countries expanded were, by definition, areas where there it was relatively easy for new people and businesses to enter into. At the time, many of the biggest changes and restructures were taking place in the 80s and 90s, many poor countries were under pressure to generate export revenue to payback international debt. The free market doctrine often pushed as part of the loan conditions by the IMF funnelled them further into agricultural and commodity goods, understood to be their comparative advantage.

> "To sum up, the producers of raw materials live in an entirely different world from that inhabited by industrial producers. ... While Bill Gates establishes the prices of his own products, producers of raw materials have to read the newspaper every day to see what the market is willing to pay them. Producers of raw materials inhabit a world close to that described by standard economic theory, with its perfect competition and with low barriers to entry"...

"The key insight by Schumpeter's student Hans Singer was that learning and technological change in the production of raw materials, particularly in the absence of a manufacturing sector, tends to lower export prices, rather than increase the standard of living in the raw material-producing nation. Learning tends to create wealth for producers only when they are part of a close network once called 'industrialism'—a dynamic system of economic activities subject to increasing productivity through technical change and a complex division of labour. The absence of increasing returns, dynamic imperfect competition and synergies in raw material-producing countries are all part of the mechanism that perpetuates poverty." (Reinert, pp. 160 & 259).

The oversupply and worsening terms of trade in these markets was inevitable, and the biggest factor in the failure of the plans of the Washington institutions various restructuring projects. As economists, the staff of these institutions should have seen it coming. Most of the goods that poor countries export are described as commodities, as they are easily graded, standardised and traded all over the world based on price. Even those goods produced by these countries that were not generally recognised as commodities often developed similar negative characteristics and poor terms of trade. These factors together generated very open and competitive markets, which in turn pushed down the level of return. As economic competition theory would suggest, if a market is oversupplied by poor country workers, prices will settle on a level just above the bare subsistence income needed to support the population of the poorest areas participating. The net result of increasing supply in these markets in which, typical to commoditised markets, demand does not increase to the same proportion when prices fall, is just lower prices and lower or frozen total revenues, which seems to have been the reality.

Reinert details the conversations he had with the president of Ecuador in 1994. The conversations took place in the middle of such a structural adjustment period for this country, and illustrate the harmful outcomes the free market policies often had.

> "In exchange for promises of large grants and loans, the Washington institutions had previously convinced him to abruptly remove industrial tariffs in order for Ecuador to specialise in supplying bananas to the world. The deindustrialisation process had lowered employment and real wages, and in fact I was there with a group organising micro-finance loans in order to help create new employment. The promised grants and loans had not appeared, the president said, and just before we arrived he had been informed that the European Union had slapped heavy import duties on Ecuadorian bananas. Ecuador is a much more efficient producer of bananas than the former French and English colonies in the Caribbean, not to mention the banana producers in the Canary Islands and Greece. By taxing Ecuadorian bananas, but not those of Europe and its former colonies, the European Union passed the cost for what were de facto subsidies for inefficient banana producers on to the most efficient, Ecuador. [President] Duran Ballen realised he had been cheated, but the manufacturing industry he and his predecessors had sacrificed was irretrievably gone." (Reinert, p. 61).

Consider the economic mechanisms and political responses in this scenario step by step. Ecuador was deemed to be one of the world's most suitable and therefore competitive locations for banana production, so therefore it should specialise and reap the rewards of comparative advantage. Ecuador is then encouraged to reduce its state support of any manufacturing industries that could not compete with the world's best, and refocus on bananas. As the free market doctrine suggests, it was to focus more of its energies on its comparative advantage, and reduce the inefficient and uncompetitive sectors that distract investment and efforts.

The structural adjustment of the country has left the banana industry in a more favourable and prominent bargaining position within the country's internal markets. The shrunken manufacturing sector is now of less importance. There are less alternative sources of work, so wages on banana plantations are not as risk of rising. There are fewer alternative areas to invest in, so the banana industry could expect to get more capital, even receiving investment into more marginal growing areas or at levels of output that are experiencing serious diminishing returns. This scenario makes the banana industry in Ecuador even more competitive, because the internal markets of the country have all been skewed in favour of this sector, and away from state-supported or protected industrialisation. Also, any demand the country now has for hard foreign currency will have to be met to a greater extent by banana exports, making the country's currency exchange rate a reflection of its relative desire for imports versus the relative desire of other countries for its bananas. This reliance on one commodity to influence the exchange rate leaves the country vulnerable to the fortunes of the year's banana crop. Ecuador's efficiently produced bananas should now displace other countries' bananas and therefore increase substantially their export income. Surely now the fruits of free trade and efficiency will accrue to Ecuador, which has been a compliant student of the Washington Consensus free market doctrine.

> "Gore Vidal, the American writer, once famously described the American economic system as 'free enterprise for the poor and socialism for the rich.' Macroeconomic policy on the global scale is a bit like that. It is Keynesianism for the rich countries and monetarism for the poor." (Chang, p. 158).

However, the rich, developed world preaches pure free trade theory only for poor and developing countries to follow, while it often makes its own economic policy decisions by different rules. When faced with the prospect of substantial changes in production and trade patterns within the banana industry, rich countries abandon the free trade ideal, and return to their alternative, more favoured domestic habit of managing competition. Despite one arm of the West encouraging free market theories for Ecuador, another side of the West's character impedes Ecuador's banana expansion through tariffs and subsidies to existing producers. The ideals of efficiency, perfect competition and free trade, when impacting upon the West's own sphere of influence, now lose out to political expediency, minor international relations objectives and the satisfaction of minor internal interest groups. In this example, the developed world has successfully convinced Ecuador to make a large sacrifice, especially in the light of the 'activities matters' themes discussed where certain manufacturing activities are good for development. It has encouraged Ecuador to stop producing state-supported or protected manufactured goods. But then the developed world has reneged on its part of the bargain, by not actually letting Ecuador dominate the world's banana markets and therefore not letting it seek a fair market reward for its sacrifice. The result is the worst of both worlds.

> "Protecting imperfect competition in the rich countries is accepted, but not in the poor. This is what I have referred to as the 'assumption-juggling' of economic theory. ... The economic power game always results in the same Golden Rule principle: the one who has the gold makes the rules." ... "others have pointed out, normal science tends to proceed within a given framework until the path has been exhausted, and then a radical paradigm shift takes place. What is special about economics is that the two parallel approaches seem to exist simultaneously.

To borrow a metaphor from American economist Kenneth Arrow, the Other Cannon tradition acts like an underground river, springing to the surface only every few decades. The existence of two parallel traditions paves the way for the opportunism and assumption-juggling we have commented on: one highbrow theory for export and a much more pragmatic theory at home." (Reinert, pp. 88 & 43).

"... Today's best advice to Third World countries is, 'Don't do as the Americans tell you to do, do as the Americans did.'' ... "Today the Chicago economists — broadly representing the theoretical foundation of the present wave of globalisation and of the Washington institutions —proclaim to the rest of the world that state and municipal governments should not intervene in the economy. In reality, Chicago's Mayor Daley spends millions of dollars of public funds establishing incubators for high-tech industries. Even in the same city, the gap between rhetoric and reality is huge." (Reinert, pp. 168 & 22).

When the economy of a developing country is 'opened up', the superior financial power and business knowledge of the rich countries enables them to cherry-pick the most profitable local businesses and markets within a poor country. This means that the areas of high profit disproportionately benefit the rich countries and profits often leave the country. They may carefully cherry-pick the sectors with the most potential for innovation and positive externalities from a poor country, and then when the domestic economy fails to grow, free market commentators unfairly cite lack of innovation as the poor country's inadequacy. Not only can a rich country cherry-pick activities, but under the guise of protecting its own businesses and jobs, a large amount of effort is made through the WTO and other legal routes to protect and fight for intellectual property rights. Much has been written on this subject by critics of globalisation, as it is easy to see how these actions can hold back development in poorer countries.

> "Economic development is all about absorbing advanced foreign technologies. Anything that makes it more difficult, be it the patent system or a ban on export of advanced technologies, is not good for economic development. It is as simple as that." ... "But the absence of protection for foreigners' intellectual property rights was often deliberate. In most countries, including Britain, the Netherlands, Austria, France and the US, patenting of *imported invention* was explicitly allowed. When Peter Durand took out a patent in 1810 in Britain for canning technology, using the Frenchman Nicolas Appert's invention, the application explicitly stated that it was an 'invention communicated to me by a certain foreigner,' then a common proviso used when taking out a patent on a foreigner's invention." ... "Today, Korea is one of the most 'inventive' nations in the world—it ranks among the top five nations in terms of the number of patents granted annually by the US Patent Office. But until the mid-1980s, it lived on 'reverse engineering.' My friends would buy 'copy' computers that were made by small workshops, which would take apart IBM machines, copy the parts, and put them together. ... At the time, the country was one of the 'pirate capitals' of the world..." (Chang, pp. 127, 133 & 11).

> "Another dysfunctional aspect of rich-country trade policy is tariff escalation: the tariffs on processed materials are higher than on the unprocessed materials. This makes it harder for the countries of the bottom billion to diversify their exports by processing raw their materials before exporting them. It hurts and impedes the development of countries that are already facing enough impediments. These are examples of 'policy incoherence' where one policy works against another. It is stupid to provide aid

with the objective of promoting development and then adopt trade policies that impede that objective." (Collier, p. 160).

"The tyranny of interlocking patents" ... "If knowledge is like water that flows downhill, then today's IPR [Intellectual Property Rights] system is like a dam that turns potentially fertile fields into a technological dustbowl." (Chang, pp. 138 & 142).

It is hoped that the many citations in these chapters will encourage further reading within this subject, and that they demonstrate that most of the points made in this section are not claimed to be very original. As a concluding analogy for the complex malign effects that rich countries have on the development of poor countries, consider the effect of a big city on the development of a nearby town, or the effect of a large supermarket on a local corner shop. The supporters of free trade ideology could say that all rich countries were once poor, and therefore economic policies should be copied. But likewise, a supermarket chain may once have been a single corner shop, a city was always once the size of a town, but that does not necessarily make it likely that the town near the city, or the corner shop next to the supermarket, will grow to equal its neighbour. In the example of the corner shop and the town, we intuitively know they will struggle to grow, so likewise we should recognise that each generation of poor countries which are attempting to develop face a different set of challenges that, by definition, the established rich countries did not face. This illustrates how flawed and condescending the advice given by the three Washington institutions can be.

The Limitations of Fair Trade Schemes

The details of fair trade schemes are not directly part of the main analysis or conclusions within this book, but the issues surrounding them sit squarely in the middle of this subject. The poor terms of trade experienced by poor country producers is a central issue in development economics, and fair trade schemes seem to be making progress in this area. But the conclusions made here propose that the fair trade schemes have their limitations when considered as a wholesale answer to world poverty. Also, the issues thrown up in this area cast another light on the themes of scarcity and supply and demand discussed elsewhere. To offer any kind of negative comment regarding these truly worthwhile and life-changing schemes seems overly negative. Therefore, firstly, it must be noted that I buy free trade products, and I am not criticising these schemes in order to discourage their current form or scale, nor wishing that they do not grow larger, which I support. I am merely suggesting reasons why they could prove to be problematic if they were to be expanded exponentially in order to become a primary answer to world poverty.

The success of the fair trade retail schemes reflects a genuine and effective response from rich country consumers to the poor terms of trade experienced by poor country producers. The markets for commodity-type goods like coffee can fluctuate up and down destructively, and have, over previous decades, periodically dropped down to levels that are very difficult for the producers – all this while the difference between a modest income and a loss for the growers can be just a few pence compared to the final retail price. Therefore, these schemes are a public recognition that, although these markets are working predictably and correctly in the economic sense, the prices resulting from the poor underlying terms of trade feel wrong on a moral level.

If the schemes are looked at from the basic economic level of supply and demand, the limitations in their ability to be rolled out further can become apparent, after a few penetrating questions are asked. Continuing with coffee as our example industry, we can test the fair trade model by considering its universal expansion.[7] First, we can ask if there is any coffee producer that would not want to be selling to a fair trade scheme. The answer is, probably no: coffee prices for members are given a floor under which they cannot fall, so probably most producers would want to join. Second, we ask if there is any coffee producer in a poor country that should not be allowed to sell to a fair trade scheme. To this, we will answer no for now, but come back to the question later. So all producers should and technically could, if the demand was large enough, be selling to fair trade schemes, and therefore all the coffee in the world could be purchased at a price that allowed for a decent income for the poor workers and farmers involved.

But we must then recognise the dynamic nature of the way people and organisations respond to prices in economies. The natural economic choices made by the other people within the population of these poor countries would lead some of these people or organisations to choose to enter into the production of coffee in the knowledge that the prices can produce an acceptable and stable income. The nature of the industry means that there is a great deal of potential human resources and land available to be diverted for the purposes of producing coffee, and therefore, in economic terminology, few barriers to entry. In countries with limited alternatives, this would inevitably lead to more potential production than was

---

[7] As Conor Woodman details in his book, *Unfair Trade*, (p55-57) unprocessed coffee prices have recently stayed well above the modest floor price set by fair trade schemes. This provides another problematic issue: companies and retailers promoting these schemes as selling points on their goods are presently not paying a higher price to the producers for doing so. As he notes, the costs to retailers of joining these schemes are presently small and the risk of them ruthlessly opting back out if price drops is a possibility.

required. Therefore, in order to prevent overproduction, as price has been inherently ruled out as a mechanism for matching supply with demand, some other mechanism for limiting supply would need to be instated. The organisations involved do not want an unmanageable surplus coffee mountain, like the EU butter mountains of a few decades ago, which were also caused by price subsidisation policies. Returning to the question above, it could be possible to discriminate between small farmers producing coffee for co-operatives and the big plantations. However, to discriminate would seem unfair to the workers on the big plantations, who may be on very low wages, and require that the large owners are paid better so they can pay them better.

This thought exercise illustrates that, as soon as the decision-making power of the natural free market has been distorted, a replacement mechanism must fill the void, whether it takes the form of production quotas or land or people-based licences. Although it must be stressed that this is not inherently negative in itself, the inevitable result of whatever replacement mechanism is used is the creation of an alternative source of value and or power. This is in contrast to the power in the market system, which is dictated only by the relative scarcity of supply and demand. The local officials, international bureaucrats, and also the rich country NGOs and corporations implementing the fair trade system, could all gain new powers from the introduction of a fair trade scheme. Can they all be trusted to act in the greater good and not abuse their new found power? In the free market system in this kind of sector, the suppliers fundamentally will have little power because there are potentially more of them than demand requires. In these commodity type markets with low barriers to entry, supply can become too abundant – therefore demand has the upper hand. The non-market fair trade solution can seek to artificially change this situation in specific cases, but as long as this is imposed on the supply side, and there are still people on the outside trying to enter this now more lucrative industry, the system can be unstable, vulnerable to corruption and problematic to administer.

It could be said that the phrase 'fair trade' has an incongruent feel about it which makes the two words seem unsuited to being next to each other. The mechanical theories and cold practicalities of trading, which are disinterested and objective, sit uncomfortably with the implied moral and subjective implications of the word 'fair.' Fair trade supporters in rich countries are motivated by the simple and admirable belief that they should pay more for goods produced by poor people, to allow them to be less poor. However, the practicalities of applying this ideal to the mechanistic characteristics of the economic markets involved requires us to challenge our notions of what we mean by 'fair.' For example, the phrase 'level playing field' is one of the most useful and effective analogies used when talking about the technicalities of 'fairness' in economic trade and competition. This phrase comes up often in situations in which one group or individual has a grievance against the situation they face in the particular market place they are in, and it conveys a complex set of assumptions and arguments in an effective and powerful way. The phrase encapsulates the idea of equity at the heart of successful capitalist cultures, meaning that, although advantages and outcomes gained by competitors may be unequal, they all do, or at least did, face the same initial market conditions that did not deliberately unjustly favour one over the other. One football team may have scored more goals, but the other team had an equal chance as the pitch was not sloping in their advantage.

As mentioned, the nub of the problem of rolling out universal fair trade schemes is that if it raises prices, and therefore rules out price as a tool to limit supply, we must then consider how else it might be possible to limit supply. There is no doubt that utilitarian principles can justify the deliberate attempt at extorting money from rich countries to poor countries by means of these schemes, but it is more problematic to use these same schemes to discriminate between which poor country producers get to participate in the market and which do not. In the free market system, this decision is arrived at through the mechanism of the system, but in contrast, the fair trade scheme inherently makes this decision a human one. This leads to the uncomfortable conclusion that the free market, low-price system, better represents some qualities of equity, as producers in theory are chosen objectively purely on the price and quality of their goods.

The greatest, largely ignored, quality of free market capitalism is that, although its outcomes are very unequal, it at least provides a relatively conflict-free way of distributing supply, demand, prices, rewards and returns. At the heart of all economic relationships, there is a conflict of interest, and it is the mechanical, disinterested resolution of this conflict which free-market economics achieves so well, at micro level at least. For example, in most areas of the labour market in a rich country, the pay rewards for various professions are not negotiated, but arrived at through supply and demand. Even when negotiations are a part of the process, the underlying values of the market represented by the supply and demand for that profession or similar alternatives provide the framework for the negotiations. The independent and objective nature of market values means the outcomes are based not on someone's opinion of the moral or theoretical worth of that person or role, but on an amoral, disinterested outcome dictated by the minimum that the employer or customer can pay, and the maximum that the employee or business can charge. Workers do not get paid what they deserve, but what they can achieve in the labour market, and submission to this more mechanical system eases and detoxifies decision making on both sides.

It may be the case that, because the world demand for certain goods like coffee is so secure and so price insensitive, and the potential good it could do to its producers is so large, that the entire market should be completely dictated by one large appointed organisation. These organisations could be practical and well-meaning islands of socialism and Soviet-style planning, going against the prevailing current of an ever-more capitalist free market world. One of the main proven downsides of Soviet-style planning is the lack of incentive, innovation and responsiveness inherent in these systems. But these weaknesses are not that relevant in this case, as good coffee beans have not changed much and are not likely to. Good coffee is good coffee, and minority niche markets always pay more and can take care of themselves. Although the wealthier countries are moving away from production subsidies towards direct subsidies in agriculture, they still have restricted markets in these areas, so the precedent for market interference is clearly there, and opposition by rich countries to such a system would appear hypocritical.

If every cup of coffee was fair trade and the world coffee market was managed and regulated by one mammoth bureaucracy, it could produce a more acceptable livelihood for those involved in the industry. That could outweigh any drawbacks, like a lack of innovation, because there is not much scope for ground-breaking innovation in coffee production anyway. As noted above, the floor for the price of coffee would have to be raised above the prevailing market price for real effects to be felt. But the point here is that we should not underestimate the power of the bureaucratic monster that will be created, along with all the potential for smuggling, corruption, favouritism, lobbying and underhanded business dealings, which typically thrive when the mechanism of the free market is replaced.

Presently, the potential for parasitic corruption off the back of the coffee growers is minimal, because they have very small margins meaning they would rather stop producing than pay any form of corruption cost. However, if the market was controlled and protected without the necessary strong leadership and discipline required to keep the process true, corruption and power politics could become endemic. By all means, the expansion of fair trade schemes could be a massively positive boost in the ending of poverty, but it is not a straightforward process. If we choose to drop the market mechanism as a method of controlling supply, which is amoral (not immoral) and disinterested (ie, not based on human value judgments), we must be willing to engage in other, more deliberate methods of limiting supply. This engagement will involve someone getting their hands dirty and making personal value judgments with life-changing consequences for competing potential regions and suppliers. In the pursuit of fairer rewards for poor country producers from rich consumers, there is a real danger that fair trade could become less fair (in the equitable sense) than free trade.

PART THREE

Where are We Heading?

CHAPTER V

The Developing Countries

As stated in the introduction, the approach of this book has been to simplify the economic world into three types of country. These are rich countries, poor countries and developing countries. The reason for this grouping originates in a central theme put forward, which is the assertion that some low-income countries are benefiting from globalisation and managing to grow, while some countries are not. The practicality of applying this distinction neatly in the case of certain countries may be problematic, but this does not detract from the usefulness of distinguishing the two groups for the purposes of discussion. Before considering where poor and rich countries are heading in the next two chapters, here the lucky few developing countries must be dealt with, as they are the key to understanding our changing economic world.

Firstly, it must be emphasised that this middle group of developing countries are the ones that are set to benefit the most from freer trade and globalisation in the recent past and near future. Indeed, much of this book is a narrative explaining how this group is winning at the expense of the other two groups of countries. In part two, conflict of interests and the zero sum nature of certain aspects of international trade set the tone. Countries like China and India are accelerating away from being merely low-cost producers, and thanks to the positive externalities they are absorbing, they are now encroaching into ever more advanced economic activities. Writing from the perspective of an established rich country, care must be taken to recognise how many lives are being positively improved by globalised trading and its subsequent industrialisation. Any concluding proposals should aim not to unduly dampen this progress. However, it is still justifiable to point out certain aspects of developing country progress that are a cause for concern.

> "Countries like China and Vietnam enter the world market for manufactured goods by paying extremely low wages. Never before has a country upgraded technologically as fast as China, accompanied by such small increases in real wages. This creates downward pressure everywhere, from Mexico to Italy. For consumers this is great news because it brings lower prices. As long as their own wages are not also sliding downwards, that is." (Reinert, p. 294)

The things that cause concern in developing countries are manifestations of the wider issues within the whole system. Inequality is a serious issue in China and India, even though in other ways they are doing very well. This new generation of developing countries have not managed to gain the more equal incomes experienced by the last generation of successfully developing countries like South Korea. When observing comparable levels of technological output, this new generation has held wages low, even for workers producing quite advanced products. Also, environmental concerns are a central obstacle to our present economic system, which is founded on a perpetual growth in consumption. These global environmental issues are highlighted more when large populations also begin to enjoy a more Western consumer lifestyle. Developing countries are also particularly prone to pollution issues, as making things is often messy, and the global division of labour has given them this role. As the dirty industrial belts and factory towns of the West clean up, the cities and rivers of China become the most polluted in the world. As cities in Victorian Britain were full of smog and filthy industrial activity, so China is now going through this passage to development. Besides environmental considerations like global warming, the physical availability of resources like water, oil, metals, and other unforeseen scarcities may prove to be the cause of bottlenecks in the patterns of development, halting the marching on of the world economy, and increasing the possibility of conflict over these scarce and shared resources.

As an aside to this theme of pollution, there is something unfair about expecting equal CO_2 concessions from countries like China, when the current international division of labour has made it the main manufacturer of goods for all developed countries. Lower-tech manufacturing production inherently involves more pollution than the type of activities currently generating wealth in the rich countries. As developing countries are making goods for those in richer countries to also consume, it appears unfair and inaccurate to label it as only their pollution. By way of analogy, excessively victimising China over causing disproportionate pollution would be like victimising the premises of a local restaurant because it used more food than the other premises in a street. Of course the restaurants use more food – it's their livelihood and we all eat there; and of course China causes more pollution, because it makes things and we all buy them.

The key point discussed later is that the growth of developing countries places an even stronger imperative on rich countries to demonstrate that perpetual economic growth, after a certain point, is not mandatory. Rich countries must recognise that their own consumption has to ease up to make the resources of the earth available for up and coming populations, and that they must lead by example on questions of the environment. While free market supporters can easily point to the fact that rich countries protecting their own economies may well limit the opportunities for developing countries, they must appreciate that factors which connect with issues of the finite nature of the Earth's resources matter more to developing countries in the long term. Protectionist policies may indeed limit export earnings in some cases, but providing a mode of economic conduct which allows rich economies not to require perpetual growth will make it more likely that middle income countries can develop and consume more. In the long term, these countries can adapt to supply different markets and even refocus on their own consumers easier than they can defy the ultimate natural constraints of the Earth's resources and tolerances. Losing a few export markets may be a blow, but fighting to consume greater resources alongside rich countries needing to do the same is *fundamentally impossible* in a world of finite natural resources and capacities. It is misled to want and justify perpetual growth in rich countries in the name of greater development for exporting developing countries.

Chapter VI

The Poor Countries

A Lesson from History on Relative Scarcity

The theme of conflict of interest has been highlighted in the issues surrounding trade and development. Conflict of interest is embedded within any economic system, and how it manifests itself and how it is resolved points towards that systems strengths and weaknesses. The following example of Britain after the Black Death episode many centuries ago is a useful one, because it reveals how the fortune of a 'class' of poor people is affected by their increased relative scarcity, compared with other factors in the economy. Economics is essentially about relative scarcities, and one of the basic lessons in textbook economics is that if something is scarce, its price goes up. This post-Black Death example is meant to further illustrate how there is a contrasting relative *lack of scarcity* of contemporary developing countries attempting to enter desirable first step international markets. As you read this section, contrast the improving prospects of the surviving medieval British peasant with the bleak prospects experienced by the contemporary poor country worker, who has been kept and led into areas of economic activity that are oversupplied and far from scarce.

The Black Death was a highly infectious and usually fatal plague type disease that swept across Britain in the mid 1300s, and killed about one-third of the population on its initial arrival. It arrived from eastern countries through the ports and spread across Britain through fleas on rats, which at the time was not well understood. Although the Black Death killed peasants and lords alike, inherently the greater absolute fall in the number of working poor people was more significant to the functioning of the economy. The widespread deaths meant that there was an unusually large and quick change in proportion between the availability of labour, and the established requirement for labour on farms and other enterprises. In textbook economic language, there was a sudden shift in the supply of labour, while the other factors of production – land, capital and enterprise – did not change as much or not at all.

In this example, the response of supply and demand to scarcity and the resulting interplay in relative power and terms of trade reveal the hidden contestable underlying forces of any economic system. The example reveals how scarcity dictates terms of trade – in this instance between classes instead of between countries, through observing what happens during a clear and abrupt change. Within a complex economy, it is often difficult to establish why values and relationships are the way they are, because competing theories cannot be proven or falsified, and because we can only see the outcome of factors and relationships. So often in economics, it is hard to prove the linkages between factors or the direction of their causation. We cannot prove which came first, the chicken or the egg. However, when a dramatic laceration to the economic system like the Black Death occurs, a window opens up to the true nature of the individual components, like the bones, joints and tendons of a body being revealed through a deep cut to the skin.

In most economic enterprises at any given time, with any given level of technology and organisation, there is an optimum mix of these factors of production required to combine most efficiently and subsequently, most profitably. For example, the efficient mix for medieval agriculture could have been one worker or serf for every three acres of land. If the same land had two men tending it, it would produce more, but the returns per worker would reduce drastically and either landowner or workers or both would be worse off. Likewise, during this time of labour scarcity, the owners of land and other businesses soon found that it was in their interest to raise wages to attract neighbouring workers in order to return their own business to nearer the previous optimum profitability levels. For example, if a landowner encountered a new ratio of one worker for every six acres on his 30-acre farm, the extra productivity to be gained from employing a new worker could be so great as to warrant higher wages. Similarly, if a blacksmith had a forge ready and waiting to do business, but he could not run it on his own, paying a higher wage would be worthwhile, in order to make both himself and his asset of the forge productive again. These basic economic laws of optimum efficiency and scarcity inevitably caused a bidding war for labour, which improved the workers' lot, without increasing the overall amount of labour available to employers.

Employers, acting in their own individually selfish way to re-establish their own former optimum mix of workers, land and capital, were unintentionally causing a shift in rewards and power away from themselves as an economic group. During this period, the increased demand for labour and the movement and flexibility it caused, helped to pull apart the established repressive feudal systems that had previously existed, and made the purely wage relationship taken for granted today more widespread. These former traditional relationships, where many of the local peasantry were tied to the local lord through a system of non-monetary obligations and traditions, were dealt a fatal blow by the increased power and choice of the now in-demand peasantry. Therefore, partly as a result of vacancies caused by death, and partly due to the increased earning power of the workers, the period was one of what we would recognise today as great class mobility, with a minority of able, hard working and/or lucky people achieving a level of change in wealth and status unusual before or in the centuries after. This meant that the structure and ownership patterns of the economy changed greatly, with the destruction of serf-lord relationships a major factor.

A revealing dimension to this period is the predictably self-preserving response of the ruling classes to this undermining of their relative power and status. This is emblematic of elites and middle-class interest groups throughout history and throughout the world, who are the most enthusiastic supporters and effective agents of free markets when they have the market advantage. But they will go to extraordinary lengths to try to avoid exposure to free markets when the market is against them, 'gaining efficiencies,' or changing the terms of trade at their cost. Predictably, in the aftermath of the Black Death, having been forced by the natural laws of free-market competition to pay more for labour due to its relative scarcity, the upper classes then tried to devise laws and regulations with the aim of restricting the peasant wages. These laws were various sorts of rudimentary income policies that tried to stem the tide of rising wages and return the larger share of the benefits of production back to the wealthy.

Also, in a way that reveals even more the petty mindset and prejudice of the way middle and upper classes often think, in certain instances the elites even devised laws to dictate how poor people should dress. These laws were intended to stop the poor people using their newfound wealth to imitate the rich and therefore undermine the status differential that all elites and middle classes have always seemed to cherish more than wealth itself. The laws dictated what kind of clothing made from what kind of material each level of society had permission to wear, with the peasantry being encouraged to wear rough wool smocks. In this way, even with the possibility of newfound wealth, no confusion could exist as to their humble origins and the superiority of the rich born man.

The example given by what happened in this period can be used to illustrate something very relevant to contemporary terms of trade debates. The terms of trade between two competing interest groups within a free market are not dictated by the wishes of either side, nor by their efficiency or productivity, but by the interplay of supply and demand in the relevant markets. Whether it is a class in society, or a rich and a poor country, the terms of trade they experience with each other are not based on the direct exploitation of the strong. The strong may win this conflict of interest indirectly by directing or limiting the economic activities of the weak to the overabundant and retaining the scarce activities for themselves, but the outcome is based on their success in controlling scarcity and not the depth and determination of their self interested power. Indeed, one of the strengths of capitalism is that it can afford to assume, and does assume, that all actors are selfish, which perhaps is the key to its survival beyond other forms of political economy. Workers always want more wages, and owners always want to pay less. Sellers always want a high price, and buyers always want a low price. Consumers all want ruthless competition in areas where they buy or employ, and protection and monopoly in areas where they sell or work.

The market forces and self-interest of the landowners of medieval Britain systematically strove to pay as little as possible for labour. In the same way, the market forces and self-interest of global trade systematically strive to pay as little as possible for goods like coffee from poor countries. However, in both cases, the wages and terms of trade are dictated by the scarcity of the inputs compared to the scarcity of the demand for the produce, not how much or how little the lords or world markets actually want cheap prices. The buyers or demonised corporations in our globalised system have no inherent ability to actually change prices or terms of trade in their favour. There is nothing built in to the underlying theory behind the free market system which dictates that the buyers who wish to achieve lower prices will succeed over the sellers wish to achieve higher prices. It is only the particular characteristics of the economic world at this point in time which makes certain trade relationships so uneven. Immediately after the Black Death episode, farms and other businesses were being run less efficiently and productively than before, when they were fully staffed in relation to the prevailing technology of the time. This, however, has no relevance to the rewards of the workers, who got more during the inefficient times than before during the efficient times. Sometimes it is preferable to be a worker in a less efficient system, because efficiency means cheapest possible price, which may refer to subsistence wages.

Today's international trade system is very productive and efficient, and is thriving, but the workers involved in poorer countries often get very small rewards, and were relatively better off a generation or two ago, when imported goods were more expensive for developed countries and fewer people and goods were involved. The drive towards mass globalisation and the many new poor countries entering into the world trading system can be effectively compared to the effects of the Black Death on the British labour market in reverse. Rather than this globalisation factor taking labour out of the production system, it is stuffing more and more in. Globalisation is making unskilled poor country labour less scarce compared to capital and enterprise opportunities. The larger narrative containing instances of restructure and opening up of economies, strong-armed by the Washington institutions during the last few decades, has pushed more and more of the world's population into supplying the same agricultural cash crops, commodities, and entry level manufacturing. The resulting worsening terms of trade are as inevitable as the improving terms of trade of the medieval British survivors above.

The Myth of Opportunity for All: Failure Built into the System

> "Keynes once said, 'the worse the situation, the less laissez-faire works'' (Reinert, p. 255).

> "And they face a high hurdle in trying to break into diversified markets for exports because China, India, and the other successful developing countries have already done so. Even once free of the traps, countries are liable to be stuck in a kind of limbo—no longer falling apart, but not able to replicate the rapid growth of Asia, and so failing to converge." ... "When will the boat come around again? That is, when will the bottom billion actually be able to break into global markets? The automatic processes of the global economy will eventually bring the boat back around. But the bottom billion will have to wait a long time until development in Asia creates a wage gap with the bottom billion similar to the massive gap that prevailed between Asia and the rich world around 1980." (Collier, pp. 95 & 86).

> "When a poor country gradually takes over shoe production, it will be close to impossible to increase the standard of living. This production is left to the poor countries, essentially because there is no more learning to be squeezed from the production process." (Reinert, p. 139).

The way that the poorest countries compete against each other in the international markets for commodities and agricultural goods, is an echo of the powerlessness of the masses Thomas Malthus observed centuries ago in industrialising Britain. The cruel dynamics of competition pushes the earning power of the weakest down to a subsistence level, as population growth and increased focus on exporting out strips the demand in these markets. Thanks to the internet, the shipping container and the growing complexity of supply chains, international price competition in these sectors is harsher than it ever was. One of the conclusions discussed earlier regarding terms of trade is that deteriorating terms of trade are often a result of many poor people seeking to enter certain economic activities, when they have limited alternatives. It can be argued that, within an environment with few economic opportunities and advantages, poor people with poor alternatives cause poor terms of trade, and not the other way around.

The terms of trade situation has been exacerbated by the Washington Consensus, because they have encouraged more and more poor countries and poor people into the same commoditised economic activities. These organisations have been promoting comparative advantage and negotiating away state intervention, including industrial policy. If these poor countries have the doors to more favourable sectors of trade closed to them, it is obvious that if they are pushed down the route of greater trade, more will pile through the door marked commodities and agricultural goods. If we were to consider all poor countries as one group, it would be reasonable to assume that they would have been rewarded for their extra productivity and effort in supplying greater volumes of commodities and agricultural goods, and also rewarded for the sacrifices and concessions made towards prioritising free markets. But the cruel caprice of the markets instead punished them through falling prices: the more they try to increase their output, the lower the prices will fall, the faster they run, the faster their competitors run.

Central to the wider ideology of the free market is the promise of greater reciprocal opportunity for countries that liberalise. The well worn line of thought emphasises that poor countries 'opening up' to free trade and allowing more rich country imports into their markets will then be able to benefit from their own opportunities to use export-led growth. However, as the post-Black Death example of the previous section demonstrates clearly, what matters to the success of one economic group is dependent on its position of relative scarcity within its markets. What matters is the volume of demand verses the volume of supply, and supply is dependent on the number of fellow competitors within your group. It is indeed correct to assert that there is a *massive* opportunity for poor countries to become successfully developing countries through international trade, but there certainly is not *universal* or *infinite* opportunity. To be able to point to a minority of countries doing well out of globalisation does not make it inevitable that every country could do the same. In fact, it is argued here that the successful countries are precisely what restrict the opportunities of the latecomers.

To accept the role of positive externalities as the source of economic progress is also to accept concentration, advantage and incumbency as central facets of economic development. In the light of the strength of positive externalities as discussed, concentration must be understood as the other side of the development coin. In the latter part of the first chapter, regional specialisation was suggested as evidence of positive externalities existing within a locality, which implies concentration. The nature of capitalist production, especially when it comes to manufacturing with its economies of scale and rich positive externalities, has well-known tendencies towards concentration. These attributes explain how the leading developing countries can build on their initial advantage to become the incumbents and achieve domination. Positive externalities are by definition about the relationships between organisations and individuals in specific locations, so location is key. When positive externalities are given credit for development, an emphasis is inherently being put on location based advantages and concepts which generate the exaggeration of small initial differences. Therefore, to value positive externalities means that a propensity for concentration and incumbency is built into the DNA of development.

Although Paul Collier could be described as a free market-leaning economist, his penetrating assertions regarding the particular subject of this chapter are very insightful and profound.

> "However before getting starry-eyed about this transformation in developing countries' trade, let us ask why it took so long. In the 1960s and 1970s the rich world dominated global manufacturing despite having wages that were around forty times as high as those in the developing world. Why did this massive wage gap not make developing countries competitive? ... But trade restrictions are only part of the explanation for the persistence of the wage gap for so long. The more important explanation is that the rich world could get away with a big wage gap because there are spatial economies of scale in manufacturing. That is, if other firms are producing manufactures in the same location, that tends to lower the costs for your firm. For example, with lots of firms doing the same thing, there will be a pool of workers with skills that your firm needs. And there will be plenty of firms producing the services and inputs that you need to function efficiently. Try moving to someplace where there are no other firms, and these costs are going to be much higher even if raw labour is much cheaper. The professional term for this is 'economies of agglomeration.' It was the key building block for the big insight of Paul Krugman and Tony Venables. They asked what would happen if the wage gap widened until it became big enough to offset this advantage from scale economies.
>
> "Imagine yourself as the first firm successfully to jump the wage gap—that is, you relocate from the high-wage world

to the low-wage world. At first you do not make a fortune. You just about break even—if by moving it was possible to instantly make a fortune, someone else would already have done so. You are the first to move and not go bankrupt, and you just get by. It is lonely being the first firm; there are no other firms around to generate those agglomerations economies, but you just hang on. And now here comes the important step. How do things look to a second firm that is thinking of relocating? Well for the second firm it all looks a bit better than it did for the first firm because there is already another firm there. So the second firm relocates. And that also helps the first firm. They both start to do better than just getting by. And the third firm? Better still. What happens is an explosive shift of manufacturing to the new location. Does this sound familiar—like the shift in manufacturing from the United States and Europe to Asia? The change is explosive because once activity started to relocate, agglomerations grew in low-wage Asia. In the process, wages are being driven up in Asia, but the gap was initially enormous and there is a huge amount of cheap labor in Asia, and so this process of convergence is going to run for many more years." ...

"It suggests to me that there was a moment—roughly the decade of the 1980s—when the wage gap was sufficiently wide that any low-wage developing country could break into global markets as long as it was not stuck in one of the traps. During the 1990s this opportunity receded because Asia was building agglomerations of manufacturing and services. These agglomerations became fabulously competitive: low wages combined with scale economies. Neither rich countries nor the bottom billion could compete. The rich countries did not have the low wages, and the bottom billion, which surely had low wages, did not have the agglomerations. They had missed the boat." (Collier, pp. 81-82 & 84).

The points Collier makes about businesses "jumping the wage gap" and relocating to developing countries echoes with the campsite analogy made earlier. It would be fair to say that at this point in time, China makes a larger and broader range of medium-technology manufactured goods than any other country in history, and its high-tech sector is progressing very quickly also. Anyone in the world with an idea for a new manufactured product would probably find the best place to start the manufacture of it would be in China, where something similar or requiring similar processes and materials is likely already being made. They would be able to find a metaphorical campsite loaded with positive externalities that suited their business needs. Filling the new factory with staff would be as simple as poaching key staff from neighbouring factories with a small incentive, and recruiting new, unskilled staff to be trained, possibly ultimately from the reservoir of the poor rural areas. The sixty-four million dollar question is: why would any potential manufacturer go to another less developed poor country, while China and India still have low wage rates? This concentration tendency is made more significant by the fact that two of the current dominant incumbent players in the most positive externality-generating sectors of trade are the two most populous countries on earth. It is challenging to be a poor country at this moment in time, aiming to develop through export-led growth, when these two giants are steaming ahead and building on their lead, and both having large reservoirs of low-income populations yet to draw upon.

To accept this state of affairs must change all perceptions of other third world poverty and development issues. Even questions of aid and trade concessions must be coloured by perceiving the world's economic environment as one of finite opportunity with only a few incumbent victors. To introduce another analogy, consider a poor country's quest for development through export-led growth as being like runners in a race. If all runners who complete a mile in less than five minutes were eligible for a prize, it would be worthwhile to assist them all in any way possible. For example, it would be worthwhile providing them all with high-quality running shoes. However, if only the top three runners were to receive a prize, equipping all the runners with high-quality running shoes will only reduce the finishing times, and not lead to more prizes being won. This zero-sum scenario, which is ingrained within the core themes discussed, is emblematic of the problems with many types of aid and development programs. The benefits of the free running shoes only reduce the times of the three race winners. Likewise, the improvements made to poor countries' production capacity only pulls trade away from other poor country producers and pulls down the market price, ie, the terms of trade.

Welcome to the State of Limbo: Stuck in the Reservoir

> "Agglomeration mechanisms are one way to explain the observed unevenness in the spatial distribution of activity and income. Development must then take the form either of mitigating the disadvantages of being outside existing centres, or of the creation of new centres of activity. What does this approach have to say about the birth of new centres? ... In the international context, Puga and Venables (1999) model the spread of an agglomeration from country to country. They suppose that world demand for manufactures is increasing (due perhaps to exogenous technical progress), and tending to widen the wage gap between countries with industry and those without. There comes a point at which the wage gap is too large to be sustainable, and manufacturing begins to move out of established centres to low wage regions. However, just one (or a few) new industrial centres will become established at a time. The logic is as we have already seen. An equilibrium with dispersed industry is unstable; any location that gets just slightly ahead of the others gains from forward and

backward linkages, these positive feedbacks causing the location to develop faster and the others to fall back. Development, therefore, takes the form of enlargement of the set of countries that are in the 'centre,' while most countries remain outside, largely unaffected. As the growth process continues, so enlargement of the set of 'central' countries proceeds sequentially, adding countries in turn. The approach predicts that development is not a process of steady convergence of poor countries to rich ones, but instead the rapid transition of selected countries from the poor club to the rich club. Which countries are most likely to make this transition? It may be determined by very small initial cross-country differences (indeed, if all countries were identical, it would simply be a matter of chance) ... The message then, is that new centres of activity can develop, but the process is not one of steady convergence of all locations. Instead, it is rapid development of a few locations, leaving others essentially unaffected. This fits well with the historical record. Recent decades have seen a small group of countries make a rapid transition from being amongst the low income group to join the middle- or high-income countries, while divergence has continued between high-income and the great majority of low income countries (Quah 1997). Furthermore, growth performance is much more variable across countries than is accumulation of either physical or human capital (Easterly and Levine 1999)." (Henderson, Shalizi, Venables, Economic development 2.2: The formation of new centres).

"Those countries that have only broken clear of the traps during the last decade have faced a new problem: the global market is now far more hostile to new entrants than it was in the 1980s. [They] ... may have missed the boat, finding themselves in a limbo-like world in which growth is constrained by external factors;" ... "When Asia broke into these markets it did not have to compete with established low-cost producers, because it was the first on the block. ... Privileging the bottom billion against low-income Asia is not just or fair; a more accurate word might be 'expedient.' Without such a pump-priming strategy, the bottom billion are probably doomed to wait until Asia becomes rich and is at a substantial wage disadvantage against the bottom billion. Even with high Asian growth, it will take several decades to open up a wage gap that is wide enough to spur firms to relocate. Only 16 percent of the cost of labour-intensive goods is, in fact, wages. So if bottom-billion wages were one-sixteenth of Asia's this would provide only a 15 percent cost advantage. You can set the meter ticking on other cost disadvantages, such as transport costs, law enforcement, corruption, electricity, and availability of skilled labor and business services. You soon get 15 percent. Remember, the Asia-OECD wage gap grew very wide before Asia became competitive with OECD." (Collier, pp. 6 & 167).

The extracts above provide an accurate picture of the situation poorer countries are in. The lucky few strike out ahead and benefit from participating in export-led growth. But many countries are locked out behind walls of positive externalities and incumbent advantage formed by the leading developing nations. Even if these remaining countries have reduced the malign influences within their economy, and even if they have reformed many of their institutions and structures, they are still stuck in what Collier describes as a state of "limbo"; not exactly a failed state, but not developing either. Within the theories of the free trade ideology, the *only* mechanism producing the dissemination of export-led growth to all the poor countries of the world, relies on the incumbent exporting country's wages rising. The theory is that the first exporting country becomes richer and uncompetitive, losing out to a poorer country when the time comes. It is important to emphasise that there are *no* other mechanisms which predict or encourage any kind of dissemination of trade to counteract the advantages of concentration. There are the vast advantages of concentration and incumbency on one side, and on the other side the only force to break this concentration is diverging wages. As Collier noted above, before the West lost much of its production abroad, wages had to reach a divergence ratio of forty to one, so a long wait may be assumed.

It seems that many of the poorest countries are to remain for a quite a while in a reservoir of limited opportunities. There is a steady flow destined for prosperity coming out of one end of the reservoir, but the flow is limited, like the controlled jet of water spouting through a dam. A water reservoir is formed when the flow of water released by a dam is smaller than the flow of the river supplying it for a period of time. Over the last few decades, more and more poor countries have been encouraged to embrace free trade, and encouraged to try to make it down the export-led growth valley, but in this case also there is a dam. The opportunity for all countries to simultaneously follow the paths that previous successful countries have followed is fundamentally not possible. This is because the nature of the relationships these growing countries need to have with the rest of the world has certain prerequisites that are finite at any one period in time. This finite opportunity, caused ultimately by the arithmetic problem above, is the dam that creates the reservoir.

To use another analogy, to claim that all poor countries of the world could all develop through export-led growth at the same time would be like claiming that families in an isolated village could all prosper by opening a shop. We intuitively understand that it would not work for an isolated village to have each house as a shop and everyone trying to earn a living as a shopkeeper. Every exporter needs an importer, and the conclusion must be that the potential for development at any one period of time is globally finite, leaving many countries waiting for their turn in a metaphorical reservoir.

This scenario recognises the possibility that even a country with good economic credentials could be left behind. This is because their failure to develop may not be a result of their own inadequacies in institutions or economic policies, or any other of the new auxiliary amendments and sub-clauses being tacked on to the free trade ideology. Instead, it is more likely that there were already enough other countries that were fulfilling the role of producer in export-led growth markets at that time. Again, let's return to the race analogy. Compare running a race where there is a prize for all those who run one mile in under five minutes to the free market interpretation, in which a country can, in the finest American tradition, create its own destiny irrespective of others. Now consider that the running race only has prizes for those who come in first, second or third, irregardless of the time. This last example is similar to the finite availability of success within this reservoir interpretation, where a country's success is a perpetually moving target and is fundamentally constrained by its environment and competitors.

Many countries are just treading water in terms of economic development, remaining on the periphery of the globalised economy. These countries can be connected to the developed world to differing degrees through trade in commodities and agricultural goods. But generally, the daily existence of these countries remains often an economic struggle to survive, as detailed forcefully in Oswaldo De Rivero's book *The Myth of Development*. The poorest countries find themselves competing with other poor countries, dealing with the fickle, turbulent and relatively overpowering nature of globalised markets from a position of financial vulnerability and relative smallness of size.

"The 1994 Rwanda genocide is generally presented to us as evil men promoting ethnic hatred ... However, this drama can only be understood in the light of the law of diminishing returns, created in this case, by increasing population pressure on arable land with almost no alternative opportunities for employment outside of the primary sector. In such a situation ... Malthusian pessimism is entirely justified."... "As Alfred Marshall, one of the founders of neoclassical economics expressed it, all migrations in history have been created by diminishing returns: an increasing density of population set off against an unchanging availability of natural resources and unchanged technology. We find this mechanism described in the Bible (Genesis 13:6) when the tribes of Israel had to part because 'the land was not able to bear them, that they might dwell together: for their substance was great, so that they could not dwell together.'".... "Under conditions of falling costs with increasing output—what we have called increasing returns or economies of scale—a large population was no longer seen as a problem for seventeenth-century economists. On the contrary, economies of scale in production and division of labour among all the new crafts made a large population a condition for economic growth ... Not until after 1798, when Thomas Malthus (1766–1834) reconstructed an economic theory built on diminishing returns in agriculture (not on innovation and economies of scale in manufacturing) did a growing population once more, as in the biblical Genesis, come to be regarded as a problem." (Reinert, pp. 157 & 71 & 74-75).

The extracts above introduce an uncomfortable and brutal truth into the subject of Third World poverty. This is that once free market ideals are disregarded, and opportunities are recognised as finite, the conclusion has to be that a growing population in poor countries is undesirable. In the past, branches of the economic establishment have asserted that

Africa's problem was too scarce a population. But Reinert's distinction between the diminishing returns of agriculture, compared with the superior labour absorption powers of manufacturing, contradict this view. If Africa cannot be expected to achieve widespread manufacturing for a few generations, the diminishing returns of its land should be borne in mind when its population is considered. Climate change is also another factor in the mix. Industrial countries can support dense populations by exporting manufactures and services, and then importing food. Countries like those in Africa have to feed themselves and also use the land to provide exports to pay for the things they need, but cannot produce. This subject is surrounded by moral controversy, but perhaps a harder approach would be kinder in the long run. Many people in poor countries view children as security in old age, so perhaps an internationally funded pension would ease population pressures.

CHAPTER VII

The Rich Countries

The End of Dominance

Where are the rich countries of the world heading? Up till now, they have done very well out of the system, being the first to benefit from the positive externalities to be found in the more favourable economic activities like manufacturing. Even since a new generation of developing countries entered the game, the logic was that the established rich countries would migrate up the technology food chain, to perform and inhabit ever more technologically advanced and innovative production and exports. The decade up to 2008 may subsequently be seen as an illusion of a golden age, where rich countries really thought they could have the best of all worlds. Did everyone really think they could perpetually have both cheap manufactured goods from countries like China, stretching their spending power and keeping down their inflation, and yet still be able to pay their way in the globalised world through high-value exports like financial services and high-end technology? This free market dream was nice while it lasted. In the hangover from that decadent binge, where many rich countries got drunk on cheap Chinese goods and cheap Chinese money, they are finding that the engines of production which drive exports and employment are not recovering as after previous recessions. Low interest rates still do not make many manufacturing businesses viable. Cash pumped into the economy does not do so much good when more of it can leak out in import demand.

In Britain, the more austere policies and the harder line taken by the Conservative-led coalition government is reminiscent of Thatcher's early 1980s. After that harsh period, Britain motored out of a slump thanks to the growing contribution of North Sea oil, the expansion of the City of London, and the mass privatisations of state utilities, which contributed to the former. In free market ideology terms, Britain was able to progress its comparative advantage by retreating from unionised manufacturing and coal mining, where it could not compete, and advancing into oil and financial services, where Britain could compete. Oil was discovered over a decade earlier, but only started contributing significantly at this time. The big bang deregulation and expansion of London's financial services sector took advantage of new digital technology and new international trends in finance. So the growth of these two sectors was possible due to factors specific to that period of time, and it is hard to see where Britain, thirty years later, can find such saviours. Oil is still significant, but not expanding, and financial services, thanks partly to the recent stupidity of some banks, are on the whole not filled with growth potential. Both of these sectors experienced a jump in significance in the 1980s, but neither is available today to perform a repeat boost to the economy.

The free market resurgence of the 1980s was able to find a new generation of comparative advantage avenues to prolong the favourable position of the rich Western countries. But in the last few decades, the development of giant countries like China and India has fundamentally changed the economic landscape. They are the ones improving their economic capabilities and increasing their consumption of the earth's resources now, and the rich countries will do well to merely maintain their current consumption. Recognising the importance of positive externalities and subsequently certain economic activities inherently helps one to understand this period of relative decline for rich countries, as well as previous periods of relative dominance. Inherent within this interpretation is recognition of the conflict of interest between countries fighting for economic advantage. As discussed above, a free market interpretation of world economics allows each country to docilely accept their present optimum economic role, but a positive externality and economic activities matter interpretation contains conflict of interests built into its DNA. To economically dominate a follower country and later to lose out to a successor country are merely two sides of the same coin and equally inevitable.

The descriptions of part one and two explain this present relative decline of the rich countries just as effectively as it explains the initial domination they enjoyed. Nothing will prove how potent rich country positive externality advantages were as well as the experience of losing a proportion of them in decades to come. What many rich countries are going through now is what relative decline looks like. And what happens when an individuals earning power drops after a long period of relative affluence? The immediate reaction is usually to build up debt as they refuse to adjust downwards their standard of living. This is what rich countries have done, and eventually it will dawn on them that a new, more modest and troubling horizon has to be accepted.

Three Trends Shaping Our Future

The tone has been set. The period of economic domination of rich Western countries is ebbing away and the new kids are on the block. The rest of this chapter will look specifically at the weak position of rich countries in dealing with trends present and growing within their economies, and why the free market solution is getting weaker by the year.

a) The Victory of the Large Company in Providing a Consumer Paradise

Most of us, wherever we live, love brand names, and as consumers and investors, we have benefited greatly from the industriousness and profit-seeking behaviour of large companies. Large companies in the right competitive environment offer consumers competitive prices and more choice, and because they value their reputation, their brands can be trusted. This may seem obvious to Western consumers, but to citizens of the Soviet Union a few decades ago, or a citizen of a less well-functioning poor country, these basic qualities and assurances would be recognised as very desirable. Indeed, the Western type of economic system is often referred to as 'consumer capitalism', and this label is very apt, as our system has served consumers quite well. As Robert Reich describes more comprehensively in his book *Supercapitalism*, those with savings of any kind have also been served well in the long term by the good management and profit-seeking behaviour of these companies. The other side of the coin that comes along with the cheaper prices and profitable investments which large companies provide is the oligarchic power that these companies command over their supply chains and employees.

> "The awkward truth is that most of us are of two minds: as consumers and investors we want the great deals. As citizens we don't like many of the social consequences that flow from them. The system of democratic capitalism in the Not Quite Golden Age struck a very different balance. Then, as consumers and investors we didn't do nearly as well; as citizens we fared better." … "Similarly, most of us value the ideal of the traditional community even while we help it wither away." (Reich, pp. 89 & 115).

Most of the factors of modern consumer capitalism favour large companies. The term business ecology is meant here to describe how businesses within a region start up, evolve and fail over time, to produce a particular mix of businesses remaining in that economy. As in nature's ecology, in business environments, there are competing pressures which together dictate whether there are many small fish in an economic pond, or a few big fish, or a nice mixture of both. In terms of small businesses, many consumers may be wistful about old-fashioned small business ecology, which is disappearing, or they may even do something about it if they are particularly passionately *into* food, music, clothes, cars, etc. But the majority of consumers, unless they have one of these passions which motivate them to buck the system and seek out the higher cost niche alternative, continue to drift towards supporting large companies. The immediate attraction of the large brand is irresistible, even if some consumers can see that they are losing something by supporting them.

Nothing emphasises the advantage of a large company more accurately than considering the benefits of positive externalities to be had by them. The mechanism of the consumer capitalist economic system does one thing very well, and that is to provide the goods that people with money want to buy, at the cheapest possible price. The advantage of large companies is absolute in many areas and their dominance is usually a one-way street. Once small family-owned shops have been replaced by a supermarket, rarely does the reverse process happen. The success of companies which bring us more value for money and the failure of those who do not, make it a one-way street of 'progress' in which comprehensively undoing or reversing the changes that have been brought about by consumer choices is difficult.

As Reich describes, large companies being a dominating presence within the economies of the Western world is not a new thing, and in some examples their power and concentration has been greater in previous times. However, it could be argued that the domination of these large companies is being perceived as being more divisive now, due them being part of the mechanism that generates more globalised trading patterns. In other words, the problem is not that large companies have become more powerful or oligarchical. The problem is that what the big companies are actually doing with their trade and production patterns is now more corrosive. For example, the car industry which Reich describes in the 1960s US was an oligarchy in which all production was within the United States, and therefore, through the well-paid jobs and the "common good" (Reich, p. 6), understanding was possible. The power and advantage these companies drew from their oligarchical position generated generally positive outcomes for, and confined to, US society.

In contrast today, the domination of economies by large companies increases their scope for partaking in ultra-competitive globalised supply chains, which have fewer fixed ties or loyalties to specific locations. They are without the option to practise any kind of "common good" behaviour due to the risk of being punished by their well-informed, fickle customers and investors. Even if it could be asserted that there is nothing inherently wrong with large companies dominating a country's economy, even their strongest supporters would have to agree that they are the agents of some of the most worrying trends in employment and trading patterns.

b) International Division of Labour—the Aristocrats, their Servants, and their Foreign Manufacturers

In Britain around the start of the last century, a surprising proportion of the workforce was employed in domestic service to the middle and upper classes. At that time, Britain was the largest investor country in the world, with the rich families of the country investing in both its colonies and in former colonies, like the ever-expanding United States. Britain also had a very productive and progressive manufacturing sector, which had earned it the label 'workshop of the world.'

Thirdly, and connected to the previous points, London had already become the lead supplier of financial services to world trade. Much of world trade took place due to finance agreed in London, on ships built in Britain and owned and insured in London. The ships often docked in London even if the goods were due to go on to somewhere else. The market prices and deals were settled in London institutions, and contracts were drawn up and disputes settled using London lawyers.

These strengths of the British economy at that time hold the reasons why Britain could afford to devote a large proportion of its workforce to supporting the lavish comfort of the upper classes. The importation of a large proportion of food consumption and other raw materials was easily financed by the export of its leading products, financial services and the earnings from profitable foreign trade and investments. In other words, because Britain had star sectors pulling in the foreign cash for imports, it could afford to pull workers away from agriculture and other such raw material industries and use them as servants. Compared to other countries without these advantages, Britain could import more of the food and other goods that these workers would have usually produced. Another prerequisite for such a high proportion of servants within a country is a high inequality of income. This was true at the time and is becoming more relevant now. As bottom-end wage costs stagnate, while the wealth of the rich grows, a growing number of service activities and occupations now become viable.

This example of Britain's upper classes getting a very good deal from the international division of labour sets the template for the free market dream existence, which many rich countries aspired to and achieved to a degree. Substitute the servants of former times with the growing service industry of present times and the pattern is very similar. Favourable trade relationships with less well-off countries mean that the rich country can pay its way in the world using a smaller and smaller fraction of its work force, and then the mechanism of progress and affluence will release ever greater numbers of surplus workers into the service industries. Although not directly employed as servants, as in former times, the low paid in the service industries create and satisfy the ever-expanding whims of those with money to spend, which improves their standard of living.

> "... the rich countries increase their real wages by successively skimming the steep part of the learning curve as new technologies become available." (Reinert, p. 143).

Nice work if you can get it! But this opulent model of existence requires a certain degree of economic and technological dominance. Contemporary rich countries seek to corner the areas of widely-traded production that are in high value-added activities, and which provide an efficient, but not necessarily secure, route to covering their trade balancing requirements (easier than making T-shirts for a few dollars a day). As Reinert suggests, rich countries attempt to inhabit areas of economic activity where productivity increases and explosions are taking place, and cede the areas of economic activity to poor countries when they become mature industries exhausted of possible innovations. This is not something which rich countries are free to choose to do, but something their high wage costs and need to pay their way in the world requires them to do. But it is an existence which appears ever more vulnerable and insecure when the rise in capability of China and co is taken into account.

On the whole, and so far up to this point, it could still be argued that this global division of labour has been generally positive for the average rich country worker. A minority of developing countries get a chance to develop, and the rich countries then redeploy their former manufacturing workers into new technology or new innovation sectors with higher returns. The growing resource devoted to the service sector equates to a higher standard of living. To be sure, trade and globalisation as a whole has made the original industrial countries better off in terms of GDP. If rich countries attempted to domestically produce all of the goods that they now import from China, it would wipe a large amount of money off their national income in one stroke. Currently, rich countries export an amount of goods and services which represents a small proportion of their national effort in terms of investment and labour, and in return (add on a little which represents the trade deficit), they receive thousands of shipping containers full of a plethora of goods made with cheap labour. The population of these rich economies could return to 12-hour work days in factories for a fraction of the pay, and still not come close to producing the goods we now consume as imports.

However, this illustrates the essential form of the dilemma in which rich countries find themselves regarding their economic structures and patterns of economic activity. As Reich describes, they are performing activities, allowing changes and making consumer choices that make them better off as consumers and investors, but by doing so, they are contributing to worrying trends:

> "We've entered into a Faustian bargain. Today's economy can give us great deals largely because it punishes us in other ways. We can blame big corporations, but we've mostly made this bargain with ourselves. After all, where do we suppose the great deals come from? In part they come from lower payrolls— from workers who have to settle for lower wages and benefits, or have to get new jobs that often pay less. They also come from big-box retailers that kill off Main Streets because they undercut prices charged by independent retailers there. They come from companies

that shed their loyalties to particular communities and morph into global supply chains paying pennies to twelve-year-olds in Indonesia." (Reich, p. 99).

The trends enacted from the tendency of consumers and investors to utilise large companies and the global division of labour has and will fundamentally change people's economic existence.

> "Fordism—understood as a system where wages increase in step with the productivity increases of the leading industrial sector—had the interesting consequence of keeping the division of gross domestic product relatively stable between labour and capital through most of the twentieth century. In my view, this kind of welfare-spiralling has, at least temporarily, largely been broken....This results from the appearance of China and India as large players in the global economy—countries that do not run fordist wage regimes ..." (Reinert, p. 145).

In other words, although India and China and other developing countries are making impressive improvements in the technology and innovation of their economic activity, they have not experienced the previously usual rise in workers' wages. Compared to equivalent periods of development in the rich western countries, the wages of the contemporary developing countries remain low. Therefore, if one has money to spend or invest, the modern world is a consumer and investor paradise, with developing countries making sophisticated manufactured goods while still employing workers on low wages. But this inevitably means that earning money for the middle and lower ranks of the rich countries is becoming more insecure and competitive. The growing power of large companies to control and squeeze their supply chains and employees, alongside the trend for manufacturing jobs to be moved to cheaper countries means that there is a downward pressure on workers' earnings in rich countries.

As Reich explains, subsequently the large companies and those who succeed within them have been encouraged to abandon their more paternalistic stakeholder mindset, and instead have been forced by ruthless competition to follow a more customer focused and purely profit-driven path.

> "When we find good deals on services, chances are we're also indirectly holding down someone else's wages and benefits in America. … If a portfolio manager in charge of my teachers' retirement fund doesn't get the best possible return on my savings, I'll switch funds. I can switch more easily now than ever before. All I need to do is click on another fund that's showing higher returns. Every fund manager knows this and acts accordingly. So indirectly *I'm* pushing CEOs to squeeze wages and benefits. I may even be pressuring CEOs to fight their unions." (Reich, p. 100).

The increase in global trade has produced a more pronounced international division of labour. The pattern is obvious and basic: rich country producers outsource or offshore areas of economic activity, which can gain advantage through using cheaper labour from abroad. This dynamic has and is changing the make-up of rich country economies. As sectors vulnerable to outsourcing or offshoring migrate, two types of sectors remain. Firstly, obviously there are a majority of economic activities that cannot be or are unsuited to being imported. The other type of economic activity that can afford to remain in a rich country must have an advantage large enough to offset cheap labour to tie it in place. These other advantages are mostly based on positive externalities, as described when considering the advantage of incumbents earlier, but now with developing countries catching up on this front, the only remaining advantage must be a high capital to worker ratio, which can achieve a technology and innovation advantage, as discussed later.

c) Our Over-Reliance on Economic Growth and Ever-Higher Levels of Consumption

The necessity of growth, not just for its own sake, but as a prerequisite for the functioning of the entire economic system, has become so accepted that it is rarely spelt out. In modern economies, as experimental efforts at greater socialism and redistribution have proved unsuccessful, and while the threatening shadow of international competition circumvents other options for equality, it is accepted that growth is a necessity. In rich countries, growth above 1 or 2 percent per year is required to prevent unemployment and poverty for the poorest sections of the population. A growth rate of zero does not indicate that next year will be the same as this year, but signals recession and unemployment. Even people and organisations with historically anti-free market capitalist backgrounds no longer openly question the importance of growth. Like a shark that needs to constantly swim to provide water through its gills to stay alive, growth is required within our rich economies – not to improve our lives, but merely to maintain the economic status quo. The wheels of the international economy must maintain and increase their unsustainable and extravagant patterns of consumption, morally underpinned by the accidental side-effect of maintaining the jobs of the relatively poor in rich countries, and making possible growth in the poor countries of the world.

This reflects a real defect in the contemporary consumer capitalist system. In this system, if the previous year's level of activity is merely maintained, there are unacceptable levels of unemployment. This system must generate extra activity just to bring unemployment down to an acceptable level. This is not the sign of a healthy, robust system, nor is it sustainable in the long run. Consider a person who has to keep putting on weight or else they get headaches. Or consider a house that has to have extra supports built onto it every year, to prevent it falling down. The conclusion would be that these scenarios were unsustainable and unstable. Also, it is important to emphasise the realities of the environmental constraints and the environmental damage incurred by rich country consumption. The perpetual growth of rich countries also appears wrongheaded when poor and developing countries are brought into the equation. This is the problem triangle at the hub of the biggest issues in the future: finite resources and environment, perpetual growth, and growing world population. This insoluble knot of conflict is so obvious and so prevalent an issue that it requires no more explanation here.

The Present Role of Technology and Innovation in Reconciling These Trends

"The historical paradox here is that it is specifically during the periods when new technologies are fundamentally changing the economy and society—as with steam in the 1840s and information technology in the 1990s—that economists turn to trade- and barter-based theories in which technology and new knowledge have no place." (Reinert, p. 57).

a) The Most Obvious Free Gift of Technology and Innovation: Positive Sum Change Which Contributes to Perpetual Economic Growth

Before considering the more subtle effects that technology and innovation have on the structure of economic activity in a rich country, it is important to first get out of the way some of the basic and obvious benefits they bestow. Inherently, if more efficient ways are found of providing goods and services, consumers of the world benefit as a whole. If a car can run on less fuel or a telephone wire can carry more information, we all benefit. If a new factory can produce a car from 100 man-hours instead of 150, either cars will become cheaper, workers will be paid more, or the company will receive greater profits. The best way to appreciate how technology and innovation have improved lives is not by looking at individual developments, but by looking back through history. Taking the long view can show just how much technology and innovation has made the lives of those in the developed world more comfortable and pleasurable. If a country's economy is managing to harness and harvest the benefits of technology and innovation within its economic activity, it will directly translate into economic development. If a large proportion of a country's economic activity is improving its ratio between inputs and outputs due to technology and innovation, and redeploying its saved inputs, this is the essence of economic growth.

Every new sector of production and consumption entered throughout history, has required that the previous, more fundamental sector become more efficient. For example, agricultural progress released people to work in factories, and factories increased efficiency and released people to work in new service-type sectors. People need food more fundamentally than cars, so if agriculture had never improved in technology and innovation, the world would still globally require most of the population to be working the land in every country. To illustrate growth achieved through the benefits of technology and innovation, imagine that in a tiny economy there are 103 people producing all the goods and services required. Then imagine that in the next year, due to improved technology and innovation applied to all their economic activity, it is found that the same amount of goods and services can be produced using only 100 people. The three now surplus people become redeployed in some new form of production or service desired for consumption by the rest of the population. Assuming the three people in this example are paid the same as the average wages, this is what 3% growth looks like, and that is how it has always worked accumulatively throughout economic history.

These types of factors of technological and innovative change within the global economy can be characterised as 'positive sum' change factors, because they generate change in which there are winners without one country or group winning at the expense of the other. This is not an instance of a zero-sum game typical to other areas of trade described earlier, but part of the universal gift of human progress. It is in these areas that Reinert stresses the optimistic prospects of industrialised economies, in contrast to the diminishing returns of activities involving nature's constraints. In this way, technology and innovation help rich countries meet their requirement for perpetual economic growth, which as shown earlier, is in the present system a necessity, not a luxury.

b) Counteracting the Trend of the Growing Dominance of Particular Large Companies

> "The world economy functions a bit like *Alice in Wonderland*, where one of the strange characters tells Alice: 'this is how fast you have to run here in order to stand still.' In the global economy, only constant innovations sustain welfare. Resting on their laurels as the world's leading constructors of sailing ships could only last until the steamship took over, when wages and employment would inevitably collapse. Schumpeter's metaphor is that capitalism is like a hotel where there is always someone living on the luxury floors, but these occupants are always changing. The world's best producer of kerosene lamps soon became poor with the advent of electricity. The status quo leads inevitably to poverty. This is precisely what makes the capitalist system so dynamic, but this mechanism also contributes to creating huge differences between rich and poor countries." (Reinert, p. 148).

Now and throughout recent history, large companies have dominated our economies, with often quite oligarchic arrangements present in many sectors. However, in defence of the current capitalist system, observers have rightly pointed out that the dynamic nature of capitalism means that it is mostly *different* companies at different times that have been dominant.

> "In 1917, Bertie Forbes, the founder member of *Forbes* magazine, published his first *Forbes* 100 list of the largest US companies. In 1987, to celebrate the list's seventieth anniversary, the magazine republished the original list and asked, 'where are they now?' The majority of the one hundred companies on the original list, sixty-one, had in one way or another ceased to exist, either merging into other companies or going bankrupt. Of the survivors, twenty-one were still around but had dropped out of the top one hundred, and only eighteen, including such venerable names as Procter & Gamble, Exxon, and Citibank, were still in the elite group.
>
> "These eighteen companies, as Foster and Kaplan note, were grand-champion survivors, weathering the storms of the Great Depression, World War II, the inflationary 1970s, the merger-and-acquisition turmoil of the 1980s, and the technology revolution of the 1990s. So they must be great performers, the truly 'excellent' companies, right? Wrong. With the exception of GE and Kodak, every one of them underperformed the average growth in stock market value during that seventy-year period, and since 1987, Kodak's performance has dropped off as well, leaving GE the sole original *Forbes* 100 company to survive *and* outperform the market over the past eight decades." (Beinhocker, p. 330).

This change at the top is rightly held up as a strength and a merit in support of our capitalist system. It shows that companies are fallible through being at the mercy of consumers, and that the established incumbent's concentration of capital and positive externalities, can be routed by a young company with new technology and innovation. The mass producing established large company can be unseated by a new entrepreneur with a new product for which consumers are willing to pay a premium. It supports the pro-capitalist view that companies serve the needs of the societies they inhabit and are exposed to consumer desires. This is in contrast to an anti-capitalist view, which would see people's interests as subservient to and controlled by large companies that create the product and then subsequently create the need. This kind of critique of capitalism often emphasises advertising as a tool used to dupe consumers, by creating new fears or insecurities which only their products can satisfy. But change at the top contradicts this conspiratorial interpretation. For example, Microsoft, Google, Apple and eBay are four of the biggest companies at the moment because they have ridden a wave of new premium consumer demand for top-rate products and services. Their technology and innovation have made the lives of many millions of people very slightly better, and in return, they have been rewarded swiftly and greatly.

If the same top 100 companies were dominant for 100 years, this would suggest a stratified stagnant economic world, where opportunities for upward mobility are very low. It would indicate that wealth and power would be very inequitably distributed, and instead actually dependent on historical incumbent advantages, reminiscent of the hereditary aristocratic landowners of the past. In support of our present system, although there is a succession of large companies dominating the company ecology landscape in many sectors, there is also still a healthy number of small companies being created. A small minority of these may succeed in using technology and innovation to 'taking out' the incumbents, which is both healthy and comforting.

Big companies enjoy notable advantages. Indeed, it is largely because of types of technology and innovation that large companies have become more successful and have been able to drive home their advantages. If someone wanted to start their own business tomorrow producing their own brand of cars, the barriers and disadvantages faced by those seeking to enter the market are prohibitively large. In 1911, it would have been a slim possibility to do so if one was able and well connected, but in 2011 it is an absolute impossibility. The only way for a new company to conquer the fortress of advantage created by the established business world is to attract the money of consumers with something new for which a premium can be charged. In markets for established goods, it will be hard to attract consumers away from the large, efficient producers, who will have economies of scale on their side. But if a small enterprise can provide a good or service that satisfies some *new* market with the application of a new innovation and or technology, then the fact that they are first on the market can trump their possible lack of advantage. Better still, if the new good or service can extend its unique selling point through intellectual property protection, then it can create time to establish itself as a new large company. In this way, new technology and innovation is a counterforce to the concentration of economic activity towards large companies, because although it often occurs within large companies, it also often occurs without them.

For this reason, technology and innovation are the main mechanisms for change in the ecology of the dominant large companies over time. The changing succession of dominant companies up until now shows this mechanism is still effective at challenging incumbents. But if the impacts of technology and innovation trail off – which is proposed as inevitable in the next section – it could be very different one day. If technology and innovation were no longer able to generate new mass-market high volume consumer goods and services, this would remove the root cause of most of the replenishment of the top ranks of companies in the economic ecosystem. The slower the changes in consumer patterns of behaviour and expenditure, the more constipated and entrenched will become the ecology of our national and international incumbent large companies. This is surely a worrying prospect and a less desirable scenario.

c) Counteracting and Reconciling the Movement of Jobs from Rich to Developing Countries by Providing a New Frontier for the Growth and Prosperity of Rich Countries

> "Those countries that are better at absorbing the knowledge inflow have been more successful in catching up with the more economically advanced nations. On the other side of the fence, those advanced nations that are good at controlling the outflow of core technologies have retained their technological leadership for longer. The technological 'arms race' between backward countries trying to acquire advanced foreign knowledge and the advanced countries trying to prevent its outflow has always been at the heart of the game of economic development." ... "Britain introduced a new act in 1750 banning the export of 'tools and utensils' in the wool and silk industries. The ban was subsequently widened and strengthened to include the cotton and linen industries. In 1785, the Tools Act was introduced to ban the export of many different types of machinery." (Chang, pp. 127 & 130).

Within the ideology of the free market, which supports greater trade and the global division of labour, technology and innovation play a central role. The central argument of the pro-globalisation project is that the trend for certain areas of production moving to developing countries, and then the goods being exported back to rich country consumers, should be allowed to run its course. The justification for this possible capitulation is the belief that the free market will then encourage the rich country's economies to redeploy their resources from these 'uncompetitive' sectors into new areas of economic activity. These new areas will be made up of either more sophisticated goods and services that may have a market abroad, or new avenues in the service sectors which will increase the countries overall levels of consumption. Technology and innovation inherently *must provide* these new areas of economic activity. It has to be technology and innovation that can provide the premium or advantage that rich country enterprises require to generate profits in a higher cost environment, as this is the *only* advantage that rich countries have to fall back on. In this shrinking world, the low costs of production in developing countries now present strong competition in many widely traded areas of economic activity, and it is only the profitable frontier of new technology and innovation which can maintain the precarious existence of being a high-cost producer. Likewise, therefore, it is only the fruits of these advantages to be gained from new technology and innovation which softens the impact of economic activity containing mature technology, seceded to developing countries.

Which of these arguments and assumptions you support will shape the way you feel about globalisation, but if you are a supporter of globalisation, your reconciliation or hope for rich countries has to rely on technology and innovation. The process of increasing a global division of labour does not just favour areas of newer technology and innovation in rich countries by not harming those enterprises, but increases their potential significance by releasing resources from the activities that are lost to competition. Sectors vulnerable to competition are hollowed out, while sectors able to compete are meant to take up the slack.

For a pro-globalisation analogy, consider a rich country containing only two factories making goods suitable for international trade, one being cups and one being satellite navigation systems. If the progress of globalisation made the cup factory close down, not only would it leave the satellite navigation system factory standing, but it would also make available the premises, workforce, capital and management from the closed factory. According to the prevailing economic ideology of our system, the growing world trade pie should lead to a higher demand for sat navs, and therefore more employees required in the world-class sat nav factory. Another fraction of the now unused resources, including employees, would end up in the service sector, helping to achieve an ever-higher standard of living for those with good jobs. In an optimistic interpretation such as would be put forward by the pro-trade ideology, the country would then be able to export the extra sat-nav systems made by half of the former cup workers in return for importing all the cups which all of the employees at the cup factory previously made.

This is an example of using comparative advantage to deploy a country's resources more productively. The output from the other half of the former cup workers would be a complete free bonus from the change when compared to the previous situation, because the original satellite navigation factory resources, plus half of the cup factory resources, have already covered the equivalent value of what all of both of the factories were making previously. These bonus workers could be deployed in the service sector, helping to increase the choices available for consumption and leisure activities.

The alternative anti-globalisation version of the same analogy might start with the assumption that the closing of the cup factory led to a greater number of workers chasing fewer jobs. In this scenario, the satellite navigation factory only wanted to take on a small proportion of these unemployed cup workers, and therefore was able to reduce its wages paid and still attract the workers it required. The capitalist investors then benefited from the lower wage costs in the satellite navigation factory, and also had the opportunity to invest in the developing country cup factory, which had even lower wage costs. Of the former cup workers in this scenario, only a small fraction can hope to gain work in the satellite navigation factory. Some will likely become unemployed, and others may go on to work in the service industry on rock bottom wages.

This analogy is crude, but it illustrates how increased globalisation can cause greater inequality in rich countries. The owners of capital benefit from lower workers' wages and now have improved investment opportunities both at home and abroad due to growing world trade. The lower relative wages in rich countries can even make new forms of domestically facing service industries become viable and existing ones now more attractive. The owners of capital and also those people of the middle class who are safely sheltered in professional jobs benefit from these changes. They experience cheaper imported goods, better investment returns and a surplus of workers to eagerly fill up service industry jobs able to satisfy their new avenues of luxury and consumption. This triple whammy makes globalisation a route to affluence and luxury for some. But in the less skilled work sectors, there is little shelter from competition, and therefore wages are pulled down.

Whether or not globalisation is viewed as good, there is no doubt that rich country survival in the present system is dependent on technology and innovation. In the analogy above, the technology and innovation of the sat nav factory is the only factor that allows the rich country to cling to its higher wages and wealth. But this insecurity of position may seem strange when we reflect how scientifically advanced rich countries already are, and how earlier we noted how much rich countries have changed the lives of their populations. In discussing technology and innovation, it is noticeable that it affects the economic system through two subtly different ways. The first is the basic eternally giving, win-win effect of progress as described earlier, while the second is more specifically related to the mechanisms and distribution of economic activity and trade. In the first form, technology and innovation provides desirable goods and services that were not available previously, or it provides an existing good or service in a way that is more efficient. In contrast to the obvious and straightforward nature of this first sphere of influence, the second is less evident and far more quietly potent.

This second sphere of influence is focused on the way that technology and innovation dictates advantage. This is revealed in the contrast in profitability between the premium of the new, and the commoditisation of the mature, or at the more extreme level, the growth and success of new products replacing old products, feeding new businesses and closing down old businesses. This boils down to how much money is spent by consumers where, and on which products, as the dynamics of technology and innovation direct the flow of the new spending power within the economy. The key difference between the two types of benefits or spheres of influence of new technology and innovation is that the first is an absolute benefit to all who adopt it forever, but the second is only of a relative and transitory benefit to those in the right place at the right time. For example, the world will have the benefit of personal computers now forever. In contrast, however, the first mass-producer of personal computers, IBM, gained large profits when it was enjoying the premium of the new as market leader and innovator, but now the commoditisation of the mature ensures that personal computers are cheaper and less profitable to the many current manufacturers. IBM is no longer the industry giant it once was, and certainly does not make much out of mainstream computer manufacture now.

The first kind of benefits of technology and innovation are permanent, but the rewards and advantage of the organisations and individuals present and instrumental at the source of the technology and innovation are transitory. Once the particular technology and innovation development is embraced, it can be used and will benefit the users forever. But in terms of the second influence, for the particular organisation or country it is merely a head start or a transitory lead, when and where a producer can gain a premium for the new for a period of time, before the commoditisation of the mature sets in. For a modern rich country to be in a healthy economic position relative to its trading partners, it is not the absolute benefits of historical technology and innovation already in action that are important, but the relative and transitory advantages given by new technology and innovation. It is the recent marginal rate and direction of movement, not the historical gain and present position. This is undoubtedly a worrying weakness when considering the far future. However much countries innovate and invent, it never will secure their affluent trading advantage for long, and with modern communication and a smaller world, that time lag is getting shorter, and the frontier of advantage getting thinner. As Reinert recalls, Alice, in *Alice in Wonderland*, was told: "This is how fast you have to run here in order to stand still."

Due to rich countries' growing reliance on the technology and innovation sectors, they need to dominate these sectors in order to survive. In the present system, this is the main source of their comparative advantage. It is not for their luxury, but a matter of economic survival. Rich countries need to be constantly pushing forwards to gain new advantages and also defending the receding of their existing advantages. It is for this reason that behind closed doors in international trade negotiations, rich countries have armies of intellectual property lawyers fighting their corner, and why in courtrooms all over the world, millions are spent on IP cases by large companies. In order to maintain a section of rich country manufacturing workers on ten pounds an hour, in the face of an accelerating developing world employing workers on twenty or thirty pounds a week, the companies and entrepreneurs of rich countries must presently continually replenish, harvest and try to protect their thinning frontier of advantage in technology and innovation, just to preserve the status quo. The concern for rich countries today, therefore, is that the quality and scope of manufacturing in low-wage countries, particularly modern China, is reaching such a high level that the concept of rich countries forever retaining a frontier of advantage is debatable.

The Uncertainty of Relying on New Technology and Innovation

The points made above demonstrate the importance of technology and innovation to the future prospects of rich countries. As demonstrated, technology and innovation can be argued to firstly check the dominance of large companies, secondly reconcile and replenish the economy after mature economic activities migrate to lower cost countries, and thirdly help to attain perpetual economic growth. It is important to emphasise how much rich countries are now totally reliant on achieving advantages in technology and innovation, as that is all they have. It has been implied earlier that trade relationships are full of conflicts of interest and can be thought of as a proxy war between countries. If this is indeed a war, then technology and innovation are the only weapons rich countries have to defend their standard of living. To revisit the distinction made earlier, it does not matter how much technology and innovation was achieved ten years ago – only new advances will replenish advantage and allow stability. Old victories mean less and less as years go by, and countries are only as good as their last few battles.

Our capitalist economies and the world economy as a whole are systems, and it is interesting to consider the weaknesses revealed by these points from a systemic perspective. The central assertion being made about the present economic system is that in order to maintain stability, perpetual change is required. That in itself is an important philosophical point to make. Rich countries presently require both perpetual economic growth and perpetual advances in technology and innovation to maintain the status quo. Most of the world has accepted the free market yoke as the lesser of many evils. As a result, most of the control over where production is located has been given up, and the dynamism of competition left in charge. Technology and innovation is the rich country's only ace card, and the only thing that replenishes the global economic system from the top. Competition is presently reshuffling the location of some of the world's production towards lower cost countries, but the process is indirectly reliant on technology and innovation giving rich countries new opportunities at the higher end to reconcile their losses.

Consider the analogy of production migrating to lower-cost countries in our globalised world as being like clothes being handed down to younger siblings. The growing eldest sibling, being the rich country, passes down his old clothes and gets new, larger clothes to wear. Everyone benefits here, but if the eldest sibling could not attain any new clothes, the system would not function. Likewise, the globalised system is reliant on rich countries gaining new areas of comparative advantage through new technology and innovation, i.e. new clothes. We supposedly understand so much about economics, but in deferring to competitive pressures, we have so little control over this economic system that we inhabit.

Free market supporters may claim that control is the wrong approach, and that countries can be confident that markets will allocate a comparative advantage to each country through the invisible hand. Many economists have spent much effort trying to explain how it is a technical and logical impossibility for a rich country to have nothing to export, as floating exchange rates would change to match the value of imports and exports. But this confidence in the benign grace of the markets was easier to have faith in when rich countries had a large lead in technology and innovation. Perhaps the technical logic of the economists is about to be reconciled by a speedy devaluing of rich country exchange rates and therefore standard of living, which may dampen the motivation to downsize and outsource? Rich countries' comparative advantage is now withering away in the face of new players like China and India. As mentioned above, one of the most widely criticised manifestations of rich country behaviour on the world stage is that of legal battles over intellectual property and other issues within the WTO. In the context of understanding the position of rich countries as explained above, it is easier to see why they are tempted to play hard and dirty in these areas. The present globalised economic system leaves rich countries fighting to stem the tide of diminishing advantage, with unemployment at stake to validate their shady actions, not merely greed.

To take a different approach to what the loss of technological and innovative advantages would mean to rich countries, it is useful to see how much they are valued in the older questions of development economics. Much of the writing and thoughts of alternative thinkers who are against the prevailing free market ideology rely on the panacea of industrial policy, industrialisation and increasing returns as an answer for poor countries. In this vein, below it is technology and innovation that Reinert claims can make economics "super-optimistic". In common with their adversaries, who support greater globalisation, an optimistic eternal spring attitude towards technology and innovation could be argued to be present in their assertions.

> "Small, poor countries often have their entire economies directed towards the export of a single product, be it coffee

or carrots. If there is no alternative employment, these diminishing returns will eventually cause real wages to fall. ... It was, in fact, this very principle that led the poet, writer and philosopher Thomas Carlyle to proclaim economics the 'dismal science.'... sooner or later society would meet the very real wall of overpopulation. This fundamentally pessimistic English economic science can quickly be made optimistic if one incorporates technological change and increasing returns. ... human society can be perceived as proceeding by forever pushing forward a never-ending frontier of new knowledge and new technology. With this vision, economics becomes super-optimistic." (Reinert, p. 154).

Reinert above seeks to emphasise the possibilities emanating from technology and innovation that can become available in a developing economy. In contrast here, the aim is to show what may happen if these factors are taken away again from a developed country, as production is lost through outsourcing and off shoring. This section marks an area of divergence from the ideas in the Reinert and Chang books that have been drawn from so heavily. Again, the divergence is based on a disagreement with the optimistic faith the two authors imply regarding the potential of technology and innovation to continue to furnish increasing returns to scale and opportunities for positive externality generating industrialisation. Once again, the interpretation here is more pessimistic. Reinert and Chang could be summarised crudely as criticising the free market ideology for making it hard for poor countries to gain from the benefits of industrialisation. The analysis in this book questions whether the gains from industrialisation could ever benefit more than a minority of countries at any one time, and in this section even questions whether rich countries can hold onto them. For Reinert to claim that economics can be "super optimistic" is to imply that technological and innovative benefits have the characteristics of being universally inexhaustible. Therefore, to deny this characteristic means that economics should be viewed as less optimistic. Proposing technology and innovation as finite brings the spectre of the dismal science back from its grave.

The following extracts give cause to doubt the ability of rich countries to achieve the globalisation panacea of finding new goods and services to export based on a perpetual technology and innovation advantage.

> "As Paul Craig Roberts says, 'Without different internal cost ratios, there is no basis for comparative advantage. Outsourcing is driven by absolute advantage. Asia has an absolute advantage because of its vast excess supply of skilled and educated labor. With First World capital, technology, and business know-how, this labor can be just as productive as First World labor, but workers can be hired for much less money.'' … "During a week of interviews with leaders of venture capital and technology firms in Silicon Valley, I found that the tech company executives are moving R&D out of the US base as fast as they can, not only for reasons of cost and quality, but also because of the link with manufacturing, which is increasingly being done abroad …

> "While they lament these trends, the CEOs and venture capitalists find themselves in the peculiar position of being pushed to move jobs and transfer technology. American thinking eschews economic strategy and offers no countervailing pressures. On the contrary, it embraces whatever the companies do as by definition the best outcome … I have spoken with hundreds of American business, government, media, and academic leaders on the topic of long-term competitiveness over the past twenty years. Their advice is always the same as Marc Andreesen's: America has to invent the next new things. This response assumes that the next new thing invented by Americans will also be

commercialised in the United States and thereby create high-wage employment for ordinary Americans." ... "For many years as the deficit in manufacturing goods rose, economists told us not to worry: Americans still had a surplus in high-tech products. In the late 1980s a special advanced technology products (ATP) category was created for US statistical reports so that this point could be easily understood. In 2001 however, that index went negative. Today [2004] the US high-tech trade deficit is over $30billion and climbing, powered by a high-tech deficit with China that has gone from nothing in 1998 to $21 billion in 2003." (Prestowitz, pp. 186, 147–149 & 129).

"Yet all is not necessarily well in Silicon Valley or elsewhere in the US high-tech establishment. The media focus on charismatic business leaders and hot new companies means that most people don't understand the real sources of technological leadership, particularly the entrepreneurial role of the US government ... Nor do people understand that technological advance usually does not come from a flash of insight but is rather the fruit of an ecosystem of interrelated companies, universities, government institutions, bankers and yes, lawyers.

"Even leading economists don't understand that if you don't have a camcorder industry you probably won't make digital cameras, either. Most of their econometric models don't account for the fact that it was easy to go into the semiconductor business when $10 million could buy you a new plant but nearly impossible now that you need $3 or $4 billion. Economists don't fully realise that if you don't think you can get a job as a software developer, you probably won't take a degree in computer science." ... "The apparently effortless technological supremacy Americans assume as a birthright is significantly based on special, transient circumstances. The two World Wars and the Cold War stimulated a massive and, for Americans, unnatural collaboration between government and industry to develop technological superiority. US domination of these industries had nothing to do with market forces and everything to do with targeted policy decisions." ... "Americans are likely to find themselves increasingly uncompetitive as individuals. They have never understood the extent to which their high standard of living has been the result of good luck rather than personal virtuosity." (Prestowitz, pp. 107, 112 & 20).

"The danger is not that countries with money will purchase American companies (directly or through their national companies)—which they will—and make off with the 'shareholder value,' which they won't. The real danger has to do with where the spillovers of innovation go. Recall that innovation has over the past fifty years provided more than half of all real economic growth in the United States and that almost all of these benefits from invention and innovation spilled outside the innovating company." ... "The Asian manufacturing nations, trying to move up into higher and higher technology and value added, are successful industrial-policy countries that seem unlikely to kick the habit, especially now that they have a fine new tool: cash, vast piles of wealth that need at some point to be moved out of dollars to be shielded from the risks of substantial exchange-rate depreciation. One shift will be into strategic investments by Asian sovereign wealth funds or national companies with access to that money to try to relocate the locus of development." (Cohen & DeLong, pp. 124 & 129).

The extracts above illustrate a concern prevalent among some economists and many business people: how will rich countries pay their way and create jobs while globalisation is ratcheting production away from them? Based on the premise that most areas of currently standard manufacturing trade were at one point in time at the cutting edge of technology and innovation, logically the production of many economic goods and services will graduate downwards to the commoditised trade realm. Few new widely traded products with a high labour input are completely immune from the possibility of being made in a lower-cost country eventually. Although goods and services that can be outsourced or offshored are a minority of any economy, they are often the most important sector in economic terms. As the extracts above conclude, it is easy to be worried by these trends, and the lofty, theory-based assurances of free market economists seem to conflict with more intuitive reasoning.

Can improvements in technology and innovation really go on for ever accelerating? The future is often defined and framed by progress in technology and innovation, and indeed the future is often presented as being a world similar to the current world, but with more technology and innovation present. Technology and innovation, therefore, could be argued to be an alternative index for delineating time within economics. This kind of approach is already signified by labels such as 'Bronze Age' or 'Industrial Revolution' or 'the digital age'. But it is important to look beyond this cliché characterisation of the future and realise that the influence of technology and innovation on the products that individuals need and buy is not infinite, but has a tendency to settle on suitable solutions to consumer needs. There is nothing inherently contained within this situation that dictates that technology and innovation will accelerate forever as it has up till now. To be sure, all successful businesses improve and fine-tune their products, but there comes a time when the changes are primarily only incremental, performed easily within the same business. This is in contrast with revolutionary changes in consumer products, which usually come from new start-up businesses, replacing and replenishing the established incumbent producers. If you look around you now and are careful to overlook the small parts of our lives that are changing rapidly, I am sure you will be able to recognise many goods and services that have 'settled' on a certain form. If I listed the goods in my flat, most would look quite similar if I tried to purchase them in 50 or 100 years.

For 300 years or more, industrialisation through the application and realisation of technology and innovation, has expanded and developed the range of goods and services available to those who can afford them – from the basics, like clothing and basic metalwork, to the remarkable, mind-boggling range of goods and services available today. Although the future is unpredictable, it is logical to assume that the biggest jump in the goods, services and conveniences available to those who can afford them has already happened. Eventually, there must be a finite quantity and range of goods and services that any person or any organisation acting in the interest of some human need or objective can ever conceivably want. It would be too easy to fall into a fallacy typical of future prediction, and just extrapolate the future as a linear continuation of the past, without thinking rationally about the nature of technology and innovation. Just because we have always existed in a world where technology and innovation are vitally important and potent factors in economic ecology and structure, this does not mean that it will always be so. After another hundred years, it is inconceivable that we will still be repeatedly finding completely new and exciting goods and services for which consumers will be willing to pay a premium on a large scale. There will always be developments in science and refinements in our goods and services, and new things on the periphery, but changes in *mass market* consumer habits will certainly one day become rarer, as we all settle on optimum goods and services in large chunks of our consumer lives.

If the notion of economic time can be assumed to be represented by technological and innovative progress, then certainly time has accelerated from the Bronze and Iron ages to its current breakneck speed since the industrial revolution. But as has been noted before, most phenomena in economics turn out to take the form of a curve, and therefore it is probable that economic time compared to real time will slow back down again. When this happens, we will have to cope and adjust to a more stagnant economic environment, similar to the Middle Ages, and this will mean fewer opportunities for rich countries to pay their way in the world. This, together with populous developing countries creeping up on the inside lane, will force rich countries to re-evaluate their free market ideology, as they have diminishing means of survival in this system. The reduced opportunities for taking advantage of technological and innovative advantage, along with developing countries' improving ability, will form a pincer movement, squeezing the life out of established rich countries. This is why the inevitability of protectionism is the main conclusion here.

Ultimately, the lubrication and dissemination mechanism for the global trade system is based on technology and innovation providing its contribution and playing its secondary role indefinitely. This analysis is proposing that this will not always be the case and is a shaky foundation for rich countries to build on. The hope, solution and sticking plaster to the shortcomings and inequalities of the present capitalist system is contained within the real potential of technology and innovation to increase and disseminate economic growth. Without this assumption, the system would fall apart. If technology and innovation ceased playing its secondary lubrication and dissemination role, and subsequently a particular distribution of the pattern of production was to be frozen forever, there would be a great change in the outlook of people in all countries.

Wherever you presently stand – rich country, developing country or poor country – the potential for changes in new technology and innovation can improve your economic outlook, and counteract the tendency of capital, positive externalities, production and subsequently wealth to concentrate and settle. To place the present time in the middle of an ongoing permanent revolution of technology and innovation means that everything is still to play for in the story of economic development. Take that interpretation away from the future, and replace it with one that predicts less change, and the future would be more hopeless and desperate for many. The ability of richer countries to stay ahead through technology and innovation underpins the utopian assumptions on which globalisation supporters rely. But this is a naïve and hopeful strategy based on shaky assumptions. If one day technology and innovation could no longer generate mass-market switches in consumption, the world economy would lose the key shuffling and dissemination mechanism required for its relatively harmonious existence. Once the eldest sibling stops getting new, larger clothes, suddenly everyone is in danger of having clothes that are too small.

The conclusion to be drawn from this chapter is that possible solutions need to be focused more directly on the needs of a static and mature economic production system, having a more tangible ability to change or resist change in production locations. Rather than relying on perpetual change in technology and innovation to ensure stability, an advanced economic system should contain the levers able to manage a static stability indefinitely. Adopting global competition that pushes and pulls resources towards their comparative advantage has served rich countries well during a period of great change. But rich countries need to graduate from a growing to a stagnant yet stable and mature stage. Selective competition-friendly protectionism is proposed as a way to help achieve this.

PART FOUR

Tempering Globalisation

CHAPTER VIII

Why Change is Inevitable

The Unsustainable Course we're Stuck On

As the last few chapters have explained, for our current economic status quo to continue, we require perpetual economic growth and perpetually greater technology and innovation developments in products exported by rich countries to aid that growth. Even if the economic world could squeeze out a few more decades of this pattern, there is still a fundamental conflict between these prerequisites for stability and environmental issues. There is no need for excessive amounts to be written here, because the issues are so obvious and widely discussed by other commentators. The fact must be recognised by even the most ardent free market capitalist that there is a conflict between a system that is absorbing a greater number of people each year and that requires perpetual economic growth, and the world's environment.

Most disturbingly, even the prospects for the very poor countries also rest on the assumption of perpetual growth of the world economy. The present basic mechanism of development requires that incumbent exporting countries like China and India grow richer, to the point where they are uncompetitive, in order to allow a new generation of exporting countries to take up the reigns. Very poor countries are stuck in an economically dormant metaphorical reservoir, or Collier's "limbo", until this happens. In the free market model it is only the excessive consumption of rich countries generating comprehensive development in the currently developing countries that will allow poor countries to become attractive as locations for manufacturing exports. One definition of economics is the study of the allocation of scarce resources, and the above-implied pattern of perpetual global growth must have serious implications for demands on the earth's resources. From a historical perspective, the scale of consumption that is required to service this type of resolution to world poverty, through geometric economic growth patterns, is very large. When the established rich countries developed, their populations numbered in the tens of millions, whereas the populations of China, alongside India and other smaller, successful developing countries, comprise around two and a half billion people. That is the equivalent to about forty Britains or eight USAs. That is a whole lot of stuff to be made and consumed.

> "We have already seen that China is the largest market for products like steel, aluminium, and cement and will eventually be the largest for many other products. This means China is beginning to inhale raw materials in the same manner as the United States ... Thus a new era of possible shortages and high commodity prices appears to be on the horizon, again with very significant economic and geopolitical implications." (Prestowitz, p. 158).

Again, it is useful to think about the world economy systematically. How does globalised trading presently work as a system for reducing world poverty? Crucially, in this proposed reservoir model we are stuck in, the solution mechanism for the end of poverty does not start with the poor getting richer. Rather, the outcome of the poor getting richer is an accidental by-product of the continued and expanding consumption of the rich. Therefore, excessive consumption is not a by-product of poverty relief, but poverty relief, in the model that best explains our current trajectory, is a by-product or unintended consequence of excessive consumption. The only tested route for poor countries to become developed in present times is through selling often peripheral and ephemeral cheap goods to rich countries. Excessive consumption is the driving force within the present ideology, and therefore progress itself is in direct conflict with environmental concerns and constraints. The issue becomes not how many resources will be necessary for the poor to be less poor, but how many resources it will take to make the rich and developing countries rich enough to buy more 'stuff' from the poor countries, to eventually make them no longer poor. Making the poor less poor has the moral substance about it to measure up to and challenge the primacy of our environmental considerations, whereas making the rich even richer is, from an environmental point of view, obscene.

Like the implied assumption dealt with in chapter seven – that rich countries require growth just to prevent their own relative poverty internally – there is a sense of inefficiency surrounding these kinds of solutions. This inefficiency is further underlined when it is recognised that greater wealth has an increasingly smaller impact on happiness as one gets richer. To use arbitrary values to illustrate the argument, it could be said that our system has to allow the rich man to get richer by £1,000 per year just to allow the poor man in the same country to get richer by £50, or even just to keep his job. Furthermore, the rich man has to get richer in order to generate more imports from poor countries. From a utilitarian point of view, this characteristic within the nature of capitalism is almost acceptable, as long as the poor are benefiting from the whole process. But the flaw in this kind of maximum utility logic is that it assumes limitless natural resources and limitless capacity to absorb pollution. In our great-grandparents' time, when human beings were fewer in number, and the world seemed abundant and vast, and as new low population colonial areas like North America and

Australia were being brought into the established trading systems, this attitude could have been justified. But since then, the exponential growth and the pervasiveness of human activity has made this presumption more unrealistic. This single environmental point has to be the biggest argument that underlines the need to change the economic course we are all on.

The last chapter discussed the role of technology and innovation in reconciling the weaknesses and conflict in the international free market system. A key point to be drawn from that chapter was that free trading pushes countries into relying on their comparative advantage more. In a system where developing countries are encroaching upon areas that used to be the comparative advantage of rich countries, the rich countries are under growing pressure to find new products and sectors. This point is a worry for many commentators in the rich countries, and, as usual, the US is the first to keenly the feel the issues. Clyde Prestowitz, in his book *Three Billion New Capitalists*, tackles these concerns head on. In the extracts below (pp. 18–20), he makes a number of potent points regarding the vulnerability of American and, by implication, other rich country economies.

> "Does manufacturing matter? In the United States, manufacturing has declined from 23 percent of GDP in the 1980s to 12.7 percent today. Europe and Japan have also seen a decline but smaller than the United States. The conventional wisdom holds that the structure of an economy, what it makes, and the services it provides are not very important and should not be the subject of government policy. According to this view, linkages between industries and technologies are unimportant, and technology development is independent of manufacturing and production. This also seems to be at odds with the realities of the third wave of globalisation."

"Economists have held it as an article of faith that high-tech manufacturing and services are done in advanced countries, while routine, low-value work is done in developing countries. But China has more semiconductor plants under construction or about to go into operation than America has. All mobile phone makers have moved most or much of their R&D to China. Nor does India limit itself to mundane software developments; it also works at the cutting edge ... US and European companies emphasise that they do a lot of high-tech work in China and India because they can't get it done as well at home."

"It has long been assumed that as manufacturing jobs disappeared, the service industries would provide secure, high-paying jobs to compensate for the loss of manufacturing. That view, however, is pre-internet and pre-third wave. It may not be sustainable in the world of three billion new capitalists all online."

"The view that the uniquely inventive US economy will always maintain economic leadership by doing the next new thing no longer necessarily holds. US spending on research and development has declined in critical areas, and its technological infrastructure is deteriorating. Other countries are graduating more scientists and engineers, while America graduates fewer and fewer. Most important, the leading US venture capitalists and technology firms are taking R&D and new start-up company development to Asia as fast as possible."

"The level playing field concept is much loved by Western political leaders who are quick to call Asian countries trade cheaters while insisting that Western workers can compete with any on 'a level playing field.' But the truth is they can't. Advanced country workers with the same skills as Chinese or Indian workers will not be able to compete

unless they are willing to accept Indian or Chinese wages."
(Prestowitz, pp. 18–20).

The above extracts voice a justifiable anxiety regarding the future, and discontent with the present free market ideology. It could be predicted that these economic truths will act as the fertile seedbed out of which support for changes to the globalisation system will grow. It is useful to understand the pressures experienced by rich countries needing to maintain their comparative advantage, as the underlying cause of other issues. For example, the vanishing comparative advantage or competitiveness in manufacturing has reduced the number of semi-skilled manufacturing jobs in rich countries, which has slewed the labour market in favour of the professional and capitalist classes. Also, the perceived criticisms of the international economic institutions, especially the contentious WTO, can be understood in a different light when we realise how perilous the situation of rich countries is within the present system. As mentioned earlier, with pressures on politicians to secure industries and jobs in the face of growing competition from developing countries, the motive is there to play hard and dirty within these international forums, and bring home the bacon for the electorate that keeps you in office. It is the weaknesses of the present system that creates these hungry insecurities, even in the face of great national wealth.

The biggest economic event of our generation has been the recent recession and credit crunch, caused by a banking crisis. But banking and financial services in rich countries, especially Britain, must be understood firstly as our great saviour in terms of a comparative advantage exporting sector. Britain was up to its neck in the world's banking crisis issues, like, for example, the American sub-prime mess, partly because the financial industry in London has become our comparative advantage. As demonstrated in the crude example of the cup factory and the sat nav factory given in chapter seven, resources in Britain are being continually released from uncompetitive manufacturing sectors and the redundant investment capital and personnel will enviably drift and be drawn into the new ventures where we are globally competitive.

This logic also explains why many established rich countries have important arms and weapons producing industries. This is a sector of the economy that has escaped the laissez-faire benign neglect allowed to happen in most manufacturing, due to its national security implications. This sector has enjoyed substantial state subsidy in the form of preferential government contracts and state-funded R&D. Indeed, the state subsidisation and support of the US arms industry, as discussed in chapter four, is a massive issue, and is often cited as a major factor in American economic success. As discussed the massive state intervention in a nominally free market country is often viewed as an example of industrial policy through the back door, disguised as something else. As a novice, it may be puzzling to hear questionable news stories about arms from respectable rich countries, which have ended up where they should not be. But when you understand these issues of comparative advantage, industrial policy advantages and positive externality effects, it is very obvious that weapons would inevitably have become a speciality of rich countries, which they are then motivated to push through trade. David Cameron does not allow arms business to encroach upon diplomatic visits to Middle East countries because he is particularly war hungry, or on the take from arms business, but because he is desperate to promote one of the few world competitive industries that we have. The more that free trade takes away other opportunities, the more sectors like financial services and the high-tech arms industry will be important to Britain's economic well being.

Britain's economy was moving towards the financial services sector when the bubble was growing. The cash that bought up the sub-prime American mortgages was cash looking for a new profit which may have metaphorically previously been invested in a factory. The idiot investment banker who was messing about in this casino may have been a factory manager in a former generation. Britain is right in the middle of this mess primarily because that is an important role that it or more specifically London has in the global division of labour, now that we are less competitive in many manufacturing sectors. The reason why the British government seems unable and unwilling to punish or hold down the bonuses of the City's financial 'talent' is that when they study the tax returns entering the exchequer, both presently and likely in the near future, they understand our country's present dependence on these businesses. The goose may have been a pain and incurred us a large vet's bill, but it is still one of the few things laying golden eggs, so we have to look after it.

In Britain, the outcome of the evolution of our comparative advantage survival has resulted in a scenario that creates bad feeling towards the economic system in multiple ways. The need to have world competitive exports has led us further into financial services, which, as mentioned earlier, was a saviour alongside North Sea oil during our crisis and transformation in the 1980s. But since the bubble and subsequent bust, the state has been obliged to step in and underwrite the banks' casino speculation, burdening taxpayers with the mistakes of the bankers. This has left very rich bankers still receiving large incomes, despite being saved by the taxpayer, while the economy suffers a very bad recession, and inequality and unemployment grows. The anti-establishment sentiments are fed by these injustices, which undermine the system and may lead to greater support for protectionism. There is a widespread feeling in both Britain and the US that relying on these artificial and speculative activities to pay your way in the world is risky, and a return to the real process, making more 'stuff', is desirable.

Taking a long term view, a rule of thumb conclusion could be drawn regarding the future of our present trade and economic system. This is that when rich countries can no longer replace sectors lost through outsourcing and offshoring, with sectors employing a technology and innovation advantage, then the whole system is in jeopardy. The end of the potency of technology and innovation advantages will cause the end of support for the free trade ideology approach. The move of Britain into the high-tech and innovative financial services sector, and equally the focus on exporting arms to oil rich countries, are typical examples of a country attempting to follow and maintain its comparative advantage. But as Britain has learnt to its cost, these sectors are risky and vulnerable, and not always the panacea they appear to be. When removing these dynamic positive sum opportunities from rich countries' economies, all that is left behind is rich countries trying to compete on price with developing countries – a situation the electorate will not be happy with. Even accepted international and political norms and historical agreements can become vulnerable to dissent, if the political pressure on governments is strong enough. The fact is that because of the issues discussed, the free trade preference of rich countries will not last indefinitely, and will inevitably be overturned when expedient for the economic prosperity and security of its voters.

A Weakened Ideology

> "The neoliberal order sought a mutual and balanced reduction of government interventionist forces. Technological and organisational progress would still be of immense value and still be realised through largely unintended spillovers from economic decisions taken for other motives. But if the logic of the market ruled, the game would at least be a fair one—in a culturally comfortable, but restricted sense of fair: minimising direct political influence on national economic outcomes. But the

neoliberal policy order is unlikely to survive this downturn intact. Governments that have been practising industrial policy will up their efforts; several others that had recently sworn off efforts will undoubtedly try again. Foreign governments may or may not succeed. They will, probably, largely fail. Technology transfer is very hard; the global economy is littered with the bones of unfit 'national champion' firms and unsuccessful government-led programs to force, via hothouse measures, the growth of commercially successful, technologically sophisticated, high-wage firms. It is, however, incontestably true that there have also been successes." (Cohen & DeLong, p. 10).

"Krugman is noted for his work demonstrating that free trade may not always be the best way for a country to raise living standards. He wrote in the 1980s that much of trade appears to require an explanation in terms of economies of scale, learning curves, and the dynamics of innovation—all phenomena incompatible with the kind of idealisations under which free trade is always the best policy. Economists refer to such phenomena as 'market imperfections,' a term conveying the presumption that they are marginal to a system which approaches ideal performance fairly closely. In reality, however, imperfections may be the rule rather than the exception." (Prestowitz, p. 181-182).

The two extracts above represent typical criticisms of the free market ideology, and suggest why free trade ideals might be overpowered by the temptation for greater industrial policy and protectionism in the future. But there is one advantage that the free trade ideology maintains over its rival theories. As echoed in the conflict and game theory points already made in chapter three, the free trade ideology provides an analysis that generates a framework at both a country level, and an analysis that suggests a framework at an international level also. In contrast, industrial policy and protectionism supporters can provide convincing analysis as to why a *single country* should follow its suggestions, but there is no stable international framework capable of holding and reconciling competing countries within a harmonious trading system. A world with zero tariffs would have its own kind of equitable uncontroversial stability, in that no bias or distortion would be present to warrant complaint. As Cohen and DeLong say above, "The game would at least be a fair one—in a culturally comfortable, but restricted sense of fair: minimising direct political influence on national economic outcomes".

This reflects a subtle advantage that free trade theory has over its opponents and why economists are attracted to its qualities. It is attractive because it can suggest a coherent international system, whereas the opposite route of protectionism can lead to a messy chaos. Some economists may envy the order found in other sciences and therefore value their beautifully ordered free market fantasy world. It is important to emphasise that there is no stable intermediate step between free trade and all-out protectionism. Once the goal of free trade is abandoned as a destination on the horizon, it is hard to substitute an alternative course that can bring order and coherence to trade relationships. Indeed, how could 'all-out protectionism' itself be defined? There is, as far as I am aware, not a clear destination where the self-interest and conflict of protectionism and industrial policy can remain at an equilibrium stasis. A theoretical situation of absolute international free trade, which has never been even remotely achieved or aimed for, can provide a stable equilibrium existence. It is stable because the trade behaviour of each member country is being dictated by the invisible hand and comparative advantage mechanisms, allowing competition to reign and organise production and trade. But move away from this absolute neat and beautiful theoretical extreme, and nothing is stable or preordained.

Given these points about the nature of protectionism, the WTO and the world trade system it tries to referee, will never ever be uncontroversial, even if it's most misled judgments from this generation are reversed. The WTO currently has an underlying remit of reducing state intervention in international trade, and moving the world closer towards the free trade ideal. As discussed, reducing state intervention is a step towards what Cohen and DeLong, above, suggested is a culturally comfortable, but restricted sense of fairness. In other words, a free trade world would be *free from* state intervention (industrial policy), and the theoretical harmony possible by everyone adopting their natural comparative advantage can be achieved. However, even if this goal was being followed in an even-handed way, which critics would certainly argue it presently is not, the goal itself is controversial due to all the flaws in the free market ideology suggested earlier and elsewhere by others. To aim for a world trade environment *free from* state intervention reveals itself to be a policy that crystallises and perpetuates the present inequality between the rich countries and many poor countries by taking away state intervention, which is their only route out of poverty.

Alternatively, if a greater acceptance of the justification of industrial policy and state intervention is adopted by the WTO in some way, the organisation may lose some of its critics in terms of its free market goals and ideology. The economists and organisations of the more left-wing and progressive persuasion would now criticise it less. However, the new, more progressive WTO would then undoubtedly invite a different type of controversy into its workings: that of countries experiencing the conflicts of interest inherent within attempts at industrial policy and protectionism. If the WTO were to retreat from its present ideology, the present central accusation directed at it – that of causing very poor countries to crystallise in their present poverty – would be avoided. But a patchwork of protectionist actions impeding the exports of different rival countries is also a recipe for international disharmony. As different national trade interests inevitably get trampled by the industrial policy or protectionism of others, many countries would feel the need to seek redress or revenge.

In other words, the stark choice is between on the one hand, a controversial goal or ideology that leads to preordained or conflict free resolutions, i.e. the free market system, and on the other hand a more sophisticated, progressive goal, but one which would invite a different type of conflict of interest into the centre of trading relations and its processes. Supporting the opinions that Reinert makes so convincingly – that economic activities are different and important regarding economic development – is to subsequently admit that at the very heart of trade relationships, there exists the basis for conflict. Different economic activities engender different development outcomes, therefore business is war and game theory type qualities apply to international relations. Perhaps the central aim of future trade theory or the remit of a reformed WTO should be to attempt to suggest or define such a situation of perceived fairness and stability, in a world where tariffs will become ever more resurgent and divisive? This propensity of protectionism for causing a conflict of interest-ridden, escalating mess, is the problem that the concept of competition friendly protectionism hopes to partially address.

The default façade of free trade ideology that most governments have used has always co-existed with examples of blatant industrial policy and protectionist aggression. As the extract by Reinert earlier suggests in contrasting the Chicago School of Economics and the behaviour of the then-Chicago Mayor, the free trade ideology has always been a convenient pick and mix affair and not a rigid, completely adhered to, ideology. Although the free trade ideology has strong characteristics, it is rarely adopted wholesale by anyone other than right-wing economists in love with its eloquence. For countries and politicians, the free trade ideology is akin to an identity. Most politicians would agree if you labelled them as being in favour of free trade, but scratch the surface and you may find that they may support regional development schemes for deprived areas, they may support subsidising investment in green projects, and they may agree with the government subsidising apprenticeship schemes where employers end up receiving free or cheap workers. These policies all break the tenets of pure free market ideology. Few politicians are ardent, pure free market supporters. Most will adopt the identity, but the reality is a convenient fudge that allows them to choose the parts to adopt or drop. Recall Reinert's extract earlier on Ecuador, where one arm of the west encouraged that country to specialise in producing bananas, and then the other arm intervened to prevent it displacing other banana producing areas. The conclusion put forward in the next chapter proposes that instead of this schizophrenic fudge, an honest and transparent approach should be taken.

People and societies have an uncanny knack of believing what they want to believe. One of the premises of Karl Marx's work was the idea that the political and economic views of a person were dictated to a large degree – whether consciously or subconsciously – by their own economic self-interest, and by their own place within the class or production system. Over the last sixty years, rich countries have done well out of the free trade ideology, but if the growth required in the present system to reduce unemployment and inequality does not materialise, voters and subsequently politicians will start to question the system. In the recent past, when the free market system has not worked for other more unfortunate countries, Western societies have been willing to swallow various spurious reasons for someone else's misfortune. In contrast, when their own situation becomes perilous, they will not swallow theoretical dogma, but instead demand change and care little about the neat and eloquent free market conclusions made by ivory tower economists.

Avoiding the Pitfalls of Protectionism

"What about trade protection on the part of the bottom billion themselves? Their own individual markets are tiny and stagnant, so focusing on the domestic market, which is all that protection can achieve, is going to get nowhere. Despite this, trade protection has been the ostensible strategy of bottom-billion governments for forty years, although its main motivation for protection was probably not strategic at all. The high tariffs induced a high-cost, parasitic industry that realised its profits depended upon lobbying rather than on productive efficiency. Globally, we now know what produces productivity growth in manufacturing: its competition. Firms hate competition because it forces them into painful changes, and painful change is what generates growth.

"Bottom-billion firms have faced very little competition. They have been protected from external competition by trade barriers and from internal competition because the domestic market is often too small to support more than one or two firms in an activity. The quiet life that the bottom-billion firms have enjoyed has been paid for by ordinary people, who have faced prices inflated above world levels by protection. That is what protection means. The quiet life has shown up in the rate of productivity growth. In bottom-billion manufacturing the rate has been around zero, in contrast to the global trend of rapid progress. Gradually, over the past two decades governments have been coaxed and cajoled into reducing trade barriers. Inevitably, when exposed to external competition these unviable activities curl up and die." (Collier, p. 160).

"As William Easterly points out every day of the week (and twice on Mondays), this [industrial policy/picking winners] is an extraordinarily risky strategy. First, it is potentially wasteful. How will a weak and corrupt government—and governments in poor countries are almost inevitably weak and corrupt—be able to channel its subsidies to just those firms whose lack of profits arises from production having temporarily raced ahead of the growth of demand? Those are the firms that will be healthy in the long run. Opposed to them are the firms that are simply inefficient. A government is not well-equipped to discern which is which. In the end, the subsidies will likely be allocated by a different principle: they will go to firms that are run by the nephew of the vice minister of finance. Thus, says Easterly, the likelihood that a country that adopts an aggressive policy of subsidising domestic industry will experience a long-term growth boom 'would seem to be pretty low.' The historical record consists not just of some East Asian countries that succeed in industrial policy but also many others that failed." (Cohen & DeLong, p. 75-76).

Collier reports a central problem experienced when countries use protectionism to create or boost domestic production. This weakness is that protectionism is fundamentally about taking away competition – and leaving businesses in environments with not enough competition can change their behaviour for the worse. Although the extracts above refer to poor countries, the threat of protectionism putting healthy competition at risk is relevant to all countries. An infamous strength of capitalism containing effective competition is that it assumes and can withstand all the actors and organisations within it being selfish and greedy. It would seem that if a country enters into protectionism, it risks losing some of these attributes.

When protectionist policies are enacted, the protected domestic markets can be too small to support production on an optimally efficient scale, and too small to support multiple producers that stay lean and innovative through healthy competition. Subsequently, the single greatest risk of enacting protectionist policies is that individual interest groups within the businesses and communities being protected choose to unreasonably increase the excess wages and profits possible under the new environment. The prevalence of capture or rent-seeking then continues to distort the signalling of prices, and therefore allocation of resources within the economic system. Subsequently, this leads to inefficient and unprogressive economic decisions being made. The outcome is often smaller-sized organisations producing lower quality goods for a local captured market. In a healthy economy, businesses need to compete for their existence according to the objective competitive factors of the free market. But protected businesses have less incentive to improve, or to challenge the interest groups that may entrench themselves within their business model. The success and continuation of the enterprise can become a subjective matter of political will, with all the conflicts of interest and corrupt cronyism that this may imply. In the worse case scenario, the protected business owners or state officials have created a cash cow with which to milk the general public, with the complicity of the state.

This weakness is exacerbated by the inherent nature of the sectors which countries usually most want to protect. Countries usually want to use protectionism to lever themselves upwards in terms of positive externalities and industrial capability. This means that each country wants to produce in a sector that gives it the best opportunity to win advantage at the upper end of its capability. But the conflict is obvious from the start, as these types of sectors inherently have small domestic markets. So the two objectives of retaining healthy competition on the one hand, and achieving a country's aspirational industrial ambitions on the other, are often set upon a collision course. To attempt to protect sectors of the economy that are pushing outwards the capabilities of that country, will inherently usually consist of smaller markets. It is for this reason that in the concluding chapter, the type of protectionism proposed is fundamentally different from the usual approach. Rather than seeking to chase the illusive new technology and innovation-rich sectors in an ambitious and combative way, the approach proposed is to protect suitable slices of more run of the mill sectors that can be large enough to sustain the reduced market scope and scale.

Whenever the subject of protectionism is brought up, some right-winger will inevitably eagerly bring up the 1930s Depression era. The world trade relations of that time are often characterised as descending into an escalating 'tit for tat' scenario, where in response to rising unemployment, each country sought to gain individual advantage, but mutual disadvantage was the result. As the previous sub-chapter discussed, protectionism does indeed point towards a chaotic conflicts of interest scenario, where national interests are easily offended and escalation, not stability, would seem to be the likely default mode of the system. A policy of protectionism aimed at improving the outcomes of globalisation would indeed have to address these issues head on. Firstly, retaliation is less likely if other countries can understand that protectionist actions derive from a general approach and a fundamental interpretation of national well being, rather than a targeted strike at certain imports.

Also, it is worth recognising that more international controversy is generated when the most cutting edge and promising areas of production are interfered with, as the presumption is that the other country wants to hog all the best bits of the world economy. In the US, much economic analysis was published about the semi-conductor market of the last few decades, as the industrial policy of other countries was felt very keenly in this emblematic high-tech sector. It is proposed that protectionism aimed at increasing equality through retaining mundane sectors will cause less controversy than a country trying to corner the cream of the manufacturing world. If protection were directed at the more mundane, mature sectors, other countries would not feel so aggrieved, especially if the implied long-term outcome was an expectation of stagnant economic wealth, instead of growing economic dominance. The bad feeling generated by perceived state involvement in the semi-conductor industry was fed by America feeling that Japan was unfairly winning this prize sector and was going to get ever richer and more powerful through these kinds of actions. If the policy instead had had the implication that it was motivated by Japan desiring less inequality and that it would cost, and not gain, it some economic growth, then probably the Americans would not have felt so aggrieved.

The arguments against employing blatantly protectionist measures can falsely paint the picture of a country moving from a harmonious, tidy free market scenario to an all-out tit for tat trade war overnight. The reality, however, is that many governments are already up to their necks in covertly trying to slew advantage towards their domestic firms, and a portion of honest and open protectionism undertaken because of inequality rather than ambitious and domineering motives, would be unlikely to rock the international trade boat that much. Countries do respect one another's right to manage their own affairs. After all, trade and friendly diplomatic relations have been successfully maintained through all kinds of economic scenarios, between countries with very diverse attitudes to economics, politics and trade.

CHAPTER IX

Competition-Friendly Protectionism

The Axis—Positive Externalities Once More, and an Explanation of Required Scope

A recurring conclusion found when studying international trade must be that generalised theories or ideological preferences are applied wholesale to the whole spectrum or gamut of international trade. But this seems simplistic when trade activity contains such diverse economic characteristics. Economists are quick to distil, disregard and simplify the extreme diversity of the characteristics of goods traded into formula-friendly 'widgets' that can be moved around eloquently in trade equations. The starting point of this chapter is to recognise that any new approach to trade must differentiate and discriminate between different traded goods, based on their fundamentally different production and market characteristics. It has been found that a diagram is the best way of representing these ideas, as there are proposed to be two dimensions of differentiation. Therefore diagram A, shown on the back pages of the book, is an attempt to illustrate how to differentiate and discriminate between different internationally traded manufactured goods. Much of the rest of this chapter will seek to explain these thoughts and ideas through the means of explaining the logic and sectors of the diagram.

The basis of this whole approach is the proposition that different goods and services have characteristics inherent within them which should influence their treatment in trade matters, and which should straddle the opposing ideological positions generally adopted wholesale by observers and economists. Practically discriminating all widely traded manufactured goods into different sectors with different propensities could offer a more sophisticated understanding of the possibilities and realities of trade intervention. This contrasts favourably with more polarised ideas and ideologies, which tend to employ sweeping generalisations about the ideal trade policy stance for a country.

Diagram A attempts to illustrate the proposition that all widely traded manufactured goods possess different endowments of two characteristics, and therefore all such goods could be allocated a position within the dimensions described on the two axes. In the diagram, the bottom axis represents the different levels of positive externalities to be had from the production of the goods in question. This axis is meant to define the difference between an economic activity that provides a relatively large injection of positive externalities into its locality, and one that does not. The examples of products given within the diagram, and the points already made regarding positive externalities in this book, should allow a good understanding of this horizontal spectrum. However, even manufactured goods with lower positive externalities available in their production compare favourably to most agricultural and commodity activities. These commodity and agricultural activities are not part of this diagram, and if they were to be included, they would appear outside the diagram's left hand side. Be careful not to confuse relatively more commoditised manufactured goods with actual commodities. The positive externalities represented here are infrastructure, knowledge and skills, networks and contacts, and creativity and diversity. These are four out of the five positive externalities discussed in chapter one. As noted in the diagram, economies of scale, which was labelled also as a positive externality in chapter one, is not included in the horizontal axis, due to the fact that it is a factor contained within the vertical axis of the diagram.

The vertical axis of the diagram represents the different market scope required for the efficient production of different products. Scope in this case means the size of the market for that product, being a combination of the number of people and the spending power they have. Different goods require different scope to provide enough demand to achieve the throughput required to attain a near optimum level of production volume. This concept requires greater explanation as, unlike positive externalities, it is not covered in previous chapters. For other types of goods or services which are not widely traded, this concept could be compared to the idea of a catchment area. For example, in the case of non widely-traded goods, it could be asserted that a supermarket requires a larger catchment area than a fish and chip shop. But widely traded goods considered here by nature do not have geographical catchment areas, and therefore this more abstract concept of required scope is used.

To illustrate the observations that make up this idea of required scope, consider the example of an imaginary bicycle factory. This imaginary bicycle factory reaches it's near optimum efficiency threshold if it produces around 100 bicycles per day. At production levels too far below this, the machinery used in manufacture remains under-utilised and the overheads of the enterprise eat into possible profits. At production volumes too far above this level, the marginal profits of extra units produced have levelled off, due to practical constraints like bottlenecks in production that may start to bite. The problems produced by higher production levels could be easily solved in the long run, but the focus here is on the problems caused by production levels too far below the optimum. The other piece of information required is how intensively people within a particular population purchase bicycles. In this example, it is proposed that the population considered make roughly one purchase for every 400 people, per year. Extrapolate the fictional values that have been suggested and useful information is gleaned. 100 bicycles x 250 working days per year equals 25,000 bicycles per year sales required in order to maintain a notionally efficient factory.

Given this kind of rough information about different products and services (and the beauty is it only has to be rough), this information could inform trade policy by suggesting how large a geographical area was required to feed a healthy, efficient and competitive market. To sustain sales of 25,000 per year, multiply this number by 400 and it can be asserted that a population scope of ten million is required. Then it can be proposed that in order to enable healthy competition between four competing rivals, a market of a minimum of 40 million people with the same propensity and income would be necessary. This is a crude example using totally fictional numbers, but it could be argued that it demonstrates a valid basic point clear to see in the economy around us. From this can be gleaned the assertion that in this fictitious scenario, a decent sized country with these market characteristics could erect tariffs in order to generate a domestic bicycle industry, without theoretically forever harming the efficiency of the industry through lack of competition. The information alone would not generate the conditions for a successful competitive industry by itself. But it would suggest that an efficient industry was at least possible. An example of an absolutely harmful trade barrier could be the market for more specialist products like a complex piece of engineering equipment, where the demand would be so sparse, as to make free worldwide trade absolutely desirable for all countries.

This concept is the starting point for the construction of the whole diagram, being that the production of all manufactured goods can be roughly given a theoretical 'threshold' size of market scope required. For example, the threshold for a certain type of population was estimated at 40 million people in the fictitious bicycle example given. This is the level of scope required to engender a near-optimum level of competition between efficiently-sized businesses. The difference in these kinds of propensities and endowments of different manufactured goods is the essence of the concepts of discrimination put forward in this chapter. In a similar spirit, Reinert (who cites Frederick List), also notes that the desirability of free trade or protectionism has no single right answer, but in this case, their interpretation is a matter not of scope but of timing for each country.

> "It is important to understand that List was both a protectionist and a free trader, depending on the stage of development of a nation." (Reinert p 161)

Likewise here, free trade or protectionism is deemed appropriate to different goods or services, depending on their demand per population propensities and the degree of scope required for their efficient production. This differentiation can demonstrate that free trade is desirable for some sectors within the diagram, where as protectionism is viable in others. It can be proposed that each good or service has its own optimum threshold of required scope, which may require a trade zone greater than the nation state or regional trade block in question, but equally, it may not.

The reason for required scope being considered so important in differentiating between different goods and services is based on notions of competition and efficiency. The concept of suitable economies of scale that increase efficiency can be understood through the description of the bicycle factory earlier. But there are other factors required for efficiency that rely not on scale, but on incentives being present. The biggest strength of capitalism is that it can and does assume that people are greedy and selfish. At its core is a minimally controversial mechanism to combat this self-interest and greed—competition. This is in contrast to communist or socialist theories, which require altruistic diligent efforts by the workers, and unselfish leadership for the common good by those with any power at all levels of organisation. This did not occur and never would occur in any possible economic society, because people are essentially more selfish than altruistic in work and financial matters. A situation where businesses are generating efficiencies and incentives through competing against one another is the biggest advantage of free market theory. In the ideal scenario, businesses compete to attract all three types of interest group in society: workers, customers and investors. The criticisms of protectionism discussed in the last chapter reveal that the protection of small markets often destroys these competitive advantages and generates corruption or cronyism. This recognition of different goods and services requiring different scope of trade in order to maintain a near-optimum level of competition is one way to begin to reconcile the conflict possible between protectionist policies and competition.

This line of thought points towards the biggest generalisation that needs to be pulled apart concerning free trade theories: that is that not all markets need *maximum* world free trade in order to meet a competition threshold. Competition is inherently good, but usually only so much of it is required to achieve its beneficial effects, and after this threshold is met, its rewards tail off. When considering most markets for goods, it is ridiculous to assume that ever-greater scope for free trade markets can continue to accrue competition benefits. The majority of markets need a certain dose of competition, but not infinite competition. It is proposed here that the nature of the production fixed costs and economies of scale in relation to density of demand should dictate an approach to trade policy, which is preferable to an inconsistent, schizophrenic trade regime dictating what is produced where. The nature of the product should inform the nature of the trade policy relevant to it.

In the diagram, four different groupings of goods and services are put forward in terms of required scope, shown as four different horizontal levels going across the diagram. This reflects the four combinations of the two different factors that are contained within a products scope requirement, being firstly the simple density of demand and secondly the fixed costs or economies of scale component within its production. As demonstrated in the bicycle example, the estimate for how large a population was required to support a protected bicycle industry was based on a rough formula that included both types of factor. The first component was the demand factor: the propensity for the population to buy bicycles, ie, one per every 400 people per year. The second component was the production factor: the level of production needed to engender efficient competition, ie 100 per day output and four competitors.

Let's return to the horizontal sections of the diagram. Firstly, in the top row, is a grouping where demand is so sparse that a large scope of market is required to generate the required level of demand, even though there are little economies of scale or fixed cost influencing this required scope level. The second row grouping comprises goods and services that require large scope markets partly or mostly because they have high fixed costs or high economies of scale. To restrict these two types of markets would put a clear absolute cost or waste on the system, as their required scope would probably be above the size of a nationally protected market. The third row grouping contains the most potent high-demand economic activities. These are markets that require little market scope, even though their goods and services have high fixed costs and/or high economies of scale. The bottom grouping still contains mass market items, but items that have little fixed costs or economies of scale within their production.

It is worthwhile to note that in giving importance to issues of scope, it seems that large countries have an advantage over small countries. Economists of all types have noted that historically, America has benefited from its large domestic market, and it could be argued that this made its past protectionism less harmful to competition. This dimension also sheds light on another advantage of colonialism, in that the colonised countries were seen as valuable markets for their European masters, as well as resource suppliers. It also adds weight to the view that mighty China is going to do well this century. In this analysis, a larger country would more often meet the scope requirements of a greater number of markets if it were considering protectionism. In the same vein, these scope issues also imply that small countries are at a disadvantage, which is why the concept of reviving or retrying regional trade zones for small economies is visited later.

A central problem that has to be mentioned with the concepts put forward in this chapter is the fact that goods and services are often not produced in ways that allow them to be neatly categorised in the way suggested. As usually found when studying economics, the real world is frustratingly messy. Often businesses make or provide a selection of products and within this selection, there may be a goods and services that fall into opposing groups in the diagram, both vertically and horizontally. The same factory may produce a best-selling line one day, and then retool its line for a very specialist low-selling line the next day, with economies of scale and positive externalities effects all connecting the different products and muddying the concepts put forward. The same company may make cutting-edge, complex products overflowing with positive externalities, and yet still be churning out the basic, mature products that it has been making for years and on which it grew its base. There is no easy defence to this flaw in the reasoning, and any interventionist government should consider this dimension carefully before enacting any policy. The differentiation concepts put forward is a limited tool that requires intelligent and careful application.

The Sectors Best Left to Their Own Devices

Free market policies are not deemed universally harmful in this book, and likewise protectionism and industrial policy have their place, but are not always useful in every circumstance. List, as cited by Reinert above, thought the applicability of free market policies was a matter of matching their timing to a country's development stage. Here the argument is that the applicability of free market forces can be understood by differentiating between the characteristics of different traded products. The analysis of diagram A suggests that three of the sectors shown should be left alone to market forces and not become part of any industrial development, or relocalisation policy.

Firstly, running along the top, sparse markets with no high fixed costs or economies of scale are best left with all the scope they can get. Therefore, free trade is the best means of achieving this. There is little temptation to protect in this sector, anyway. Secondly, sparse markets with high economies of scale are more efficiently left to global suppliers, and these would naturally often be developing industrialising countries performing 'emulation', as is now the case. Finally, the requirements of the pioneering small business sector suits a free market environment, with all its superior searching capability, in contrast to a state policy, which may have a poor ability to 'pick winners' and may generate little potential payoff in terms of economies of scale when a good product is hit upon.

But as the details of past economic domination discussed earlier should have explained, a business selling in a relatively free market can still have inherited many non-free market advantages. So even though the small business sector is best treated as a free market in terms of its products, this does not mean the sector is not open to advantages from non-free market elements. As noted in the diagram, past and present

R&D spending to enhance the local business environment and ecology is more significant in this small business sector, and it is this that should be monitored if comparisons are to be made about the true extent of a country's industrial policy depth. This would be where the US, despite claiming to adhere to only the invisible hand, would be revealed as a big interventionist player, thanks mainly to its massive defence budget.

The Prize Sector: Wake up and Smell the Coffee, Name the Game and Share out the Spoils

This sector is where international conflicts of interest and game theory concepts really count. A central message of earlier chapters was that industrial policy can be very potent in certain circumstances, and the prize sector within the diagram represents the areas of international trade where this fact is most pronounced. As mentioned, the reason why US academics published so much about the Japanese state support of its semi-conductor industry a decade or more ago was because it exemplified the characteristics of a prize sector. It was high fixed cost, cutting edge, high turnover, full of positive externalities and very dynamic. Positive externalities are important in all aspects of economics and production, but in this prize sector, it must be appreciated that they can be development rocket fuel for developing and rich countries alike. Economic activities more modestly endowed with positive externalities can still pump some progress into a country's environment, but it is this sector that can really boost developing and rich countries' business ecology, with high-end positive externalities.

Taking the lead from Reinert and Chang, the aim here has been to encourage rich countries and the US especially to *get real* about why they are so prosperous, and to give up the expedient façade that free market policies alone have been responsible for their good fortune. Once the truth is accepted regarding how great a role industrial policy and positive externalities have had in historical development, then a more penetrating scrutiny and honest bartering of industrial policy can be aimed for, perhaps even through the likes of the WTO. Possibly the greatest benefit and legacy the WTO could bestow on the world would be not the reduction of tariffs, but an intellectual and practical framework for calculating the entitlements or equivalent effects of various countries' tariffs as they resurge. The basis of this mode of thought is that if, as claimed, industrial policy within the prize sector can be identified as a golden goose for the countries concerned, then in the interests of international fairness and harmony, these 'geese' need to be recognised for what they are, and perhaps even shared out more overtly. In past generations, it was obvious that the minority of rich, developed countries would corner the cream of economic production and markets, but as the capability of other countries catch up, this division of labour can no longer be taken for granted and some monitoring and sharing mechanisms must inevitably develop.

Traditional industrial policy supporters may question why aggressive industrial policy within the prize sector is not put forward as an answer to different countries' problems. The reason is that, although this is the most important sector of trade, its character is often not suited to the particular objective proposed here, which is to provide steady jobs and a tightening of labour markets. As Easterly would lead us to believe, the planning bent of states would often not be agile enough to search out and replicate the best product or business models in this fast-moving sector. Also, the most prized parts within the prize sector are already pretty crowded, and to advise more countries to attempt to jostle in on this action seems unwise and naive. For example, listen to politicians discussing the future of industry in any rich country, and I would bet that it would not be long before some kind of nod was made towards investing in renewable energy or electric vehicles. This is an admirable sector to subsidise, but seen from a distance it would seem foolish for *all* the countries concerned to believe that their nation will be disproportionably successful or competitive exporters within this sector.

It is being proposed here that as more and more countries develop, the prize sector will become ever more crowded, transient and insecure, and will not be large enough to employ the number of people required to maintain a reasonable degree of equality and social cohesion within rich countries. The prize sector markets often will not be large enough to flourish if protected, and also the nature of enterprises in this sector mean that they are inherently too fast-moving to make state intervention pay back worthwhile benefits. Free market supporters will often mention the tit for tat trade disputes of the 1930s as an argument against protectionism. As mentioned, there is indeed an insecure dynamic present in protectionist natured trade relations, which is a further reason to keep protectionist policies away from the most desirable sectors, such as those within the prize sector. Protectionism used in a way that hurts the most high tech and prized sectors in other countries, can easily sour international relations. But using protectionism in a way that does not involve attempting to increase your own share of the cream of global economic activity, and which furthermore expressly reduces a country's own economic growth, is less likely to incite retaliation from other countries.

Prize sectors are absolutely great for countries and for the whole population of the world. They are the drivers of economic growth and technological and innovative progress, and they produce the pinnacles of human achievement. But they simply are no longer generating a great volume of jobs in our new offshored, outsourced and internet-linked world. Be amazed at the products, enjoy the products, hope that your country is involved in producing at least some of the products, but do not base all your country's future jobs requirements on the hope of only producing products in this sector. The prize sector is the answer to many questions and problems, but not this jobs issue. In fact, as suggested by the thoughts in chapter seven, there is reason to assume that the prize sector will shrink as a proportion of rich country economies, as the provision of goods and services 'settle' on stable forms of products, and subsequently technology and innovation lose their potency in mainstream economics. It is easy to over-focus on high-tech and innovative enterprises and forget that most of the things we spend our money on will not have changed radically in fifty years.

The Relocalisation Sector: The Least Worst Way to Achieve Progressive Goals

This section details the main conclusion of this book – that there is a case for using competition-friendly protectionism for progressive reasons. As is usual, protectionism for the chosen products here means using state intervention in the form of tariffs or import restrictions to disadvantage imported competition. As Diagram A and this chapter have sought to demonstrate, the diverse goods and services traded between countries contain different characteristics of relevance to protectionism issues. The conclusion here is that it is only goods deemed to fall within this sector of the diagram which are viable for competition friendly protectionist policies. This is firstly because in order to qualify as being 'competition friendly', the market protected must be large enough to generate competition based on only domestic demand. Therefore, this implies the bottom half of the diagram only. Secondly, the bottom right hand quarter of the diagram is deemed to be populated with products and industries which require and generate a high degree of cutting-edge technology and innovation, unsuited to the cumbersome and long-term nature of protectionism. These industries are also becoming less and less capable of generating the number of secure jobs required of such a policy intervention. Also, as discussed, protectionism in this desirable quadrant would be too controversial internationally, inciting retaliation from other countries. Therefore, the bottom left hand quadrant is the relocalisation sector, where it is proposed that a few relatively more stable, high-volume markets can be protected to achieve progressive goals.

There are many questions and factors connected to this proposition of competition-friendly protectionism, and therefore this sub-chapter covers a lot of ground. Discussed in this section are: why protectionism is desirable, why it is viable in certain cases, why its economic costs can be bearable and worthwhile, how people will react to it, a note of warning about the policies being abused, the way the policy applies to poor countries, and finally, a lead-in to the next sub-chapter regarding intermediate trade zones for poor countries. While this section is quite theoretical, some further practical considerations regarding the form and actual implementation of such policies are discussed in the last sub-chapter.

What are protectionist policies pushing against? One of the broad conclusions of earlier sections is that the factors that generate development, and the factors that generate the concentration of production or provision of certain goods and services, are two sides of the same coin. Find an economic environment that generates development, and you also have the recipe for concentration. Identify a country which has an advantage in a certain industry due to positive externalities or 'agglomerations' or economies of scale, and you have also identified the disadvantage of other, less able countries to enter that market. As explained, in some economic activities, positive externalities kick in and provide an advantage as soon as this specialisation starts to form in a location. Development and the economic activities that best generate development contain the propensity to concentrate hardwired into their DNA. In a world of finite opportunities, this concentration or the advantage of the incumbent is what locks some countries out of the development club, and leaves them to remain festering in the economic reservoir or Collier's "limbo". The dynamic of the present world is leading towards a concentration of industrial production in leading developing countries such as China and India, with both rich and poor countries on either side of the development spectrum experiencing problems of lacking opportunity and growing inequality as a result.

Therefore, given this propensity for concentration, the counter force of relocalisation or competition friendly protectionism is proposed in this sector as a way to rebalance economies and achieve progressive goals. It is not *maximum* efficiency and incentives or *maximum* competition that should solely be the goal of economics, but other goals, like the dissemination and distribution of the economic activities that encourage and support development, should be considered. Remember that the primary source of economic development is positive externalities, and these will *never* spread into the very poor countries of the world if their economies are forever passed over due to them never being the ideal locations for production. For this reason, it can be argued that other goals, such as the relocalisation of production nearer to where it is consumed, and the greater equality produced by tightening labour markets, are positive outcomes in themselves. If we are aiming to combat global poverty and inequality, the act of breaking these concentrating forces inherent within industrial capitalism should be a component of a forward-looking approach to economics.

Consider the following proposition as an argument for relocalisation and in answer to the usual label given to protectionism, which is that it is a zero-sum (or worse) activity from an international perspective. The value of the positive externalities generated by a business organisation producing a particular product is not directly correlated to the size of the enterprise in a straight line, but is, like most things in economics, proposed to be a curve. For example, an enterprise producing thirty sofas per year generates very few positive externalities – a small fraction of its turnover. In contrast, a furniture factory producing three thousand sofas per year could be creating a massive injection of positive externalities into the locality, of a far larger value in proportion with its turnover. However, it would be reasonable to assume that there would be a diminishing level of positive externality generation if the furniture factory would keep on expanding indefinitely. At some point in the production level, the ratio between turnover and positive externalities generated would reach an optimum amount per unit of turnover, and then begin to decline.

This logic can be used to assert that in certain situations, the value of having two locations generating positive externalities for two regions can be greater than one location that is double the size. In other words, after a certain threshold of size is met for the market for that product, dissemination carries an absolute economic benefit in the form of greater positive externalities produced in total. This concept of diminishing positive externalities in relation to enterprise size can be used as a direct economic argument for the dissemination of industry between countries, even counterbalancing some instances of minor efficiency and incentive losses. This logic demonstrates that even if industrial policy or protectionism is indeed the act of countries fighting over finite markets, the process of splitting the location of production or provision can, *if the market is large enough*, increase the total positive externalities produced. You will be reminded, as mentioned earlier, that studying positive externalities is unrewarding for the professional economist, because the subject can only yield generalisations and obtuse logical assertions such as the above, and not the detailed falsifiable empirical proof and economic laws which are more greatly prized by the profession.

Besides the above economic argument for the relocalisation of industry, the moral case for using competition-friendly protectionism as a vehicle for improving equality and reducing poverty is strong. The mechanisms and incentives of free trade provide maximum economic growth due to maximum efficiency savings and maximum incentives. These free market policies, therefore, can rightly claim to create the largest possible international market of goods and services. However, as the free trade liberalisation model succeeds in providing increasing total economic growth, the marginal benefit of that growth for the rich must eventually diminish, as for every individual, extra wealth has increasingly less marginal value. Also, if this growth is produced by a system that also generates inequality, many of the positive effects are cancelled out by the negative costs of inequality. Unequal societies often have poorer social cohesion and therefore have to spend more on costs such as jails, police and private security. The argument that free market liberalisation produces maximum growth in some instances will never be disproved, but the point will just become less relevant to contemporary economic problems and environmental constraints. There is a trade-off between equality and total efficiency, and somewhere along this line, everyone will adopt a socialist viewpoint. It is not an absolute question, but one of degrees. As wealth in rich countries gets higher and reaches the stage where consumption by many is arguably too high for environmental reasons, it will be hard to justify continually gearing the economy towards traditional economic growth. There are very few ways for a person to spend extra wealth which do not have a negative environmental impact.

This argument can allow possible answers that reduce or impair the economic growth of the capitalist system, but any such measures must be limited and retain the right incentives, or a disaster like the attempts at communism may result. Given these points, it is not the degree to which new policies take an economic society away from the maximum free market consumption that matters, but the retention or replacement of the free market system's incentives and mechanisms. Any change must replace or retain the relatively unsubjective and uncontroversial systems of allocation and conflict resolution which are so important, and which competitive capitalism does so well. Losing or foregoing a large swath of wealth from the wealthiest sections of the population would be acceptable, but doing so in a way that harmed the incentives, efficiency and conflict resolution of the whole system would be unacceptable. This is why the practical differentiation between products seems useful, and why the term "competition-friendly protectionism" is used.

It is fine for free market supporters to assert that growing the cake should be the economic priority, and splitting the cake should be the moral afterthought. But as it is clear to observe, charity, state benefits or aid to poor countries are no substitutes for home-generated development or the honest, wholesome merit of being a fully contributing member of a well-functioning economic ecosystem. If we maximise the cake and seek to maintain poor countries and poor sections within rich countries on aid or benefits, those societies will continue to adopt the negative dependency and corruption that aid critics and social commentators note. This chapter proposes that the dissemination of production and positive externalities should also be a goal of international economics and trade, and that differentiation can point to what kind of markets should be allocated for this goal, and more importantly, which markets should not.

Free market economists will react violently at the mention of protectionism, and probably begin extrapolating what they propose to be the net cost in wealth of diverging from the free market optimum. And they will be partly right: protectionism will destroy wealth. They may also worry about the high cost of protected products for consumers. But this latter issue is not such a good case, as societies already pay high wages for the provision of certain goods and services that have to be produced domestically. Increasing this grouping by adding economic activities that were previously performed in low-wage countries will be a significant anomaly in trade policy, but will not feel revolutionary in terms of day-to-day economic reality. The extra demand for domestic unskilled labour will contribute to a 'tightening' of the labour market which will also affect the wage costs of non-protected sectors. This tightening will increase wages as long as immigration is controlled. As comparative advantage trade theories would dictate, consumers within the protected area would lose a greater monetary amount than that which was gained by the workers, but the equality advantages gained could help to increase cohesion and improve values within society. The prospect of reduced inequality and decent paid jobs available would allow the ethos of the value of being a working man or woman to be raised, and also allow more severe targeting of benefit dependency and petty crime.

The analysis within this diagram is proposing that the important factor in considering the use of protectionism is not the loss in total wealth for the country concerned, and in the case of already rich countries, need not even be based on positive externality arguments, but that required scope should be the guiding prerequisite. If protectionist policies make the resulting market scope for the product protected too small, the outcome maybe inadequate competition. As correctly identified by protectionisms' detractors, this situation may cause absolute losses in efficiency and incentives, and even interest group 'capture'. But to get it right and protect a product within a market area that contains above the threshold of required scope for that product, the protection activity need not harm the valuable competition. If the market protected is large enough, even after protection it will maintain the valuable efficiency, incentives and conflict resolution qualities that competition provides. If the threshold level of scope is met after a protectionist policy is implemented, the policy merely becomes a transfer of income to the less skilled in society, from the more skilled. There will still be an absolute loss in national wealth paid as the price, as dictated by comparative advantage theories, but these need not be terminal or disruptive to the orderly workings of the economy. Remember the post-Black Death example from chapter six, where the tightening of the labour market reduced inequality. There is no reason why such a tightening in rich countries could not be manufactured by trade policy alone.

As a note of warning, in parallel with such a policy development the potential for abuse must be recognised. Along with tightening a country's labour market, the greater restriction of trade's union activity of labour on the one hand and competition policy applied to capital owners on the other must be enacted. The greater equality objectives desired must sprout from a *general tightening* of the free and flexible labour and business markets, and not by special interest capture like union activity or companies colluding. Beware of ideologically-driven socialist elements within society taking the ideas too far, which they *will* try to. Incentives and efficiency will be under-appreciated by these elements in society, who will be just as quick as the free market ideologues to forget large parts of why rich countries are so rich and productive. It could become part of the healthy political debate to choose how far to go down the protectionist and relocalisation route, weighing up as a society the loss in national wealth that this anti comparative advantage stance would cause. Also, strict controls for 'dumping' onto unprotected markets need to be part of the implementation. Depressingly, it may be found that a country requires a degree of unemployment and restraint on these progressive policies in order to prevent excessive inflation or decadence. But still, the conclusion must be that in rich countries, the relocalisation of production through protectionism could be the least worst way to buy equality with wealth, as long as the economic activities are chosen carefully to have the right combination of mass market demand to engender a competitive, healthy business ecology.

The concept of the reservoir earlier has illustrated why most poor countries will not accede to becoming developing countries in one large wave, but a few at a time, and many not for a generation or two. In the meantime, while waiting for their turn in the metaphorical economic reservoir, a relocalisation policy pushing specific labour intensive production into poor countries must be the least worst outcome for the present. Again the stress must be on choosing robust economic activities which will engender a competitive business ecology. Poor countries are more susceptible to corruption; therefore, the questions of scope in order to provide competition to kill off corruption are even more important. Research and local knowledge would be required to help choose products to protect and relocalise in specific countries, but the guidelines provided here at least give a framework to use in making these choices. In the past, poor countries have tried to reach for the super-positive externality star enterprises straight away, but have failed to reach a critical mass of competition and development. In contrast, the concepts here suggest protection is better targeted at more modest mainstream mass market goods, where stunning technological leaps forward or export-led growth is not to be expected, but modest job creation and small steps towards a healthy stable economy can be made.

The main problem poor countries have when considering questions of required scope is the smallness of their economies. As Collier points out, the borders of many African countries result from the whims of colonial history, and now often still combine small populations with low incomes. This smallness of their economies makes reaching a required level of scope for specific goods or services very hard. The demand for a product is a factor of not just population, but a population and its wealth, and therefore poor countries with ample population size may still lack the required scope of market purchasing power required to make protecting a particular economic activity viable. Products that may be universally consumed in rich and developing countries could be the preserve of the rich in poor countries. Protecting these small markets for progressive objectives may easily lead to corrupt and backward outcomes as Collier characterises. These factors lead to one well trodden conclusion. Small, poor countries should create regional trade groupings in order to create a trade area that can be large enough to allow protected activities a healthy required scope or market size. This is the subject of the next section.

Creating Intermediate Scope Markets: Reattempting Regional Trade Agreements Between Poor Countries

This conclusion of regional trade blocks for small, poor countries being part of a solution is a well-trodden path and completely not original. Therefore, extracts from favourite economists are employed below.

> "Africa is being divided into a complex network of areas with different trade agreements—the so-called spaghetti bowl—in which the EU and the USA try to increase their fields of interest. The map of these trade agreements is not very different from the one resulting from the Berlin conference of 1884 ... Small African industrial markets are not integrated into a larger market that might have industrialised Africa. Instead, industrial Africa is increasingly fragmented, and while some countries are better off than

others, each market is relatively open to the killing competition from the North." (Reinert, p. 62).

"List argued for the formation of an intermediate continental free trade area before globalisation. This is the step that Latin America never took: the Latin American Free Trade Association (LAFTA or ALALC) was a failure. Latin America's import substitution strategy was initially very successful—even the small Central American countries achieved growth around 10 per cent for a long time—but it degenerated into superficial industrialisation and monopolistic competition..." (Reinert, p. 285).

"Manufacturing in the bottom billion is in decline. Thirty years of protection created a parasite with stagnant productivity, and a decade of modest liberalisation has merely reduced its size. ... There, [Africa] exporting really does appear to raise productivity. Domestic markets are too small to support much competition, and so learning from exporting is differentially powerful. We found it was a big effect: whereas the norm for African manufacturing was stagnant productivity, exporting got a firm on a productivity escalator. So if Africa, and by extension the other bottom-billion economies, are to get a dynamic manufacturing sector, it is more likely to come from breaking into export markets than from going back to the years of cosy domestic monopolies. The problem is how to get firms over that initial hump of competitiveness and enable them to get on the escalator." (Collier, p 166-167).

The regional free trade zone that Reinert mentions may have provided a suitable market exposure and incentive for the small protected industries within these countries. This may have been the ideal intermediate step between the protected inefficiency of small producers in small markets and the complete free market exposure to the world's strongest players, which has happened under the Washington Consensus regime.

"If we had allowed these middling industrial economies—like Peru and Mongolia—to develop their industries through protection, gradually integrating them with their neighbours, some day they could have become strong enough to compete in a global free market. Instead, neo-classical economic theory has figuratively bombed Mongolia 'back to the Stone Age', to use an American expression from the Vietnam War." …. "The sudden loss of volume caused by the shock therapy killed scale-based activities, shielding only activities subject to constant and diminishing returns (the traditional service sector and agriculture). This interconnectedness of factors explains why experience-based economic theorists. … stress the importance of gradualism in matters of free trade." (Reinert, pp. 164 & 171).

This is a central conclusion found in Reinert's book. Regional trade agreements should provide the missing step between the small scope of a poor nation state and the maximum scope of free world trade. Given that his and this book's starting premise is that economic activities contribute differently to development, and given that free trade affects what a poor or developing country can competitively produce, an intermediate stage of free trade with other similar countries is preferable as an alternative. As discussed, Reinert stresses that the desirability of free trade for a country is a factor of degree and timing regarding its development, not an absolute for or against. Trade is beneficial for small economies to increase the scale and scope of their markets in order to increase economies of scale, competition and choice. But this is preferably achieved by degrees over time, only when the country is ready. Having free trade relations only with countries of similar development level to your own for a certain period of time is a crucial missing middle step that, although it is an old idea, so far poor countries have not been able or allowed to get right.

> "... deindustrialisation can lead to the opposite of development, to retrogression and economic primitivisation. One of the mechanisms contributing to this is the Vanek-Reinert effect, which causes the most advanced economic sectors in the least advanced trading nation to be the first casualties of instant free trade" ...."... modern international trade theory insists that free trade between a Neolithic tribe and Silicon Valley will tend to make both trading partners equally rich. Other Canon trade theory, on the other hand, insists that free trade is beneficial to both parties only when they have both reached the same stage of development."... "The German economist Friedrich List theorised about the timing of tariffs and free trade. ... [stage] (3) a period where ever larger geographical areas would be integrated economically. ... It is important to understand that List was both a protectionist and a free trader, depending on the stage of development of a nation. ... Moving directly from List's stage 2 to his stage 4 had the same effect on Latin American manufacturing as if suddenly subjecting a greenhouse plant to a cold climate. [The] manufacturing industry died out, and the lack of demand from the manufacturing sector prevented these economies from upgrading their knowledge-intensive service sector in the way it happened in the rich countries." ... (Reinert, pp. 166, 66, 161-162).

Collier provides a more negative and right leaning critique of regional trade integration.

> "For forty years, the politically correct solution to bottom-billion trade problems has been regional integration. ... Such schemes have not accomplished much, however. One reason is that even in the best-case scenario, the resulting markets remain tiny. A famous statistic is that the whole of sub-Saharan Africa has an economy about the size of Belgium's. A second reason is that if you combine a number

of poor, slow-growing individual economies, you have a poor, slow-growing regional economy. Trade is really generated by differences, and the big opportunity for low-income countries is to trade with rich countries, harnessing the advantage of their cheap labour. Worse, the differences that do exist between poor countries will get reinforced rather than reduced." (Collier, p. 164).

Issue can be taken with a few points that Collier makes here. Firstly, if trade is "really generated by differences," why is most rich country trade with other rich countries? Rich country trade patterns suggest that positive externalities, like spatial economies, agglomerations, economies of scale and the rest of the points discussed in part one are involved, not just factor cost differences. These positive externalities are central to poor country development; therefore, not only are cost differences only part of the picture, they are a less important part of the picture in terms of development potential. It could be argued that a country attempting development through trade generated only by cost differences is less likely to succeed than a country attempting development through the other advantages generated by creating new positive externalities.

Secondly, criticising a regional trade grouping for being slow-growing is only relative to the alternative of not having the arrangements. Slow growth is better than no growth, and furthermore, in this analysis, present short-term growth is secondary to the aim of increasing longer-term positive externalities within the domestic environment. The first generation of slow growth achieved through moving slowly into manufacturing could prove to be more beneficial in the long-term than a fast spurt of growth achieved through resource extraction or a temporary commodity boom. Thirdly, if a regional trade grouping of poor countries produces leaders and followers, surely the rules of the free trade ideology must kick in to require the lead country to import something back from the follower country. Only envy could prevent a poor country from preferring to lose out in trade interests to its neighbour rather than through globalisation in general, which is happening at present. As Collier demonstrates in his section on landlocked countries, at least a neighbour's growth may spill over into your own home country, or improve your access to world markets.

The rich and powerful countries have always controlled the patterns of world trade, and regional trade groupings made up only of poor countries is against the rich countries' own economic interest and therefore has never been supported adequately by them. Also, these trade groupings would require a sustained political focus and co-operation over many years to design and manage, something which poor countries find hard to achieve. Regional rivalries, ethnic, religious and political tensions, and even outright military conflicts can all play their part in scuppering the best laid plans. Some commentators label the poorest countries with the greatest problems as being "failed states". Given the fragile and ineffectual nature of the governance of some of these countries, it is little wonder that regional trade groupings have never succeeded. Only through international support employing rich country political pressure and finance could any such plan ever work, but a unified agreement on the form of such a plan would be difficult.

Summary: Differentiation not Ideology

The basis of this proposed approach to trade and protectionism is a process of differentiation between the vastly different characteristics of goods being internationally traded. This differentiation contrasts sharply with many economists and commentators, who often reach general conclusions about international trade, through discussing products or characteristics of products, which would fit only in certain sectors located on the diagram. Free trade economists can be found guilty of assuming that all traded goods benefit from the extra economies of scale provided by having a larger market, but as discussed earlier, this is a generalisation and not a rule. Some widely traded goods have domestic markets of an adequate size already to enable healthy domestic competition. Anti-free trade economists can be found guilty of assuming that protecting high-tech goods with small domestic markets will not have any negative lack of competition side effects and that every country can pursue this kind of approach without generating international systemic equilibrium problems. In other words, if every country is pursuing export-led growth, who is importing all the stuff? This approach seeks to qualify both these standpoints, pointing out where each of their arguments may fit and where they may not.

For example, could Collier's views on protectionism gone wrong be argued to apply only to the upper half of diagram A? Could it be asserted that mass market goods with dense demand could overcome the problems he describes? In other words, Collier's anti-protectionism stance rests mainly on the proposition that it is deemed to cause corruption and cronyism due to inadequate competition. But this presumption that all markets protected will always be too small to enable competition is a generalisation that need not be inherently true of all protected goods. Collier was observing bottom-billion countries with very small economies, which obviously is an important factor in issues of market scope. Also, there is a tendency for states to attempt to use protectionism to aid more prestigious enterprises, which are often slightly too ambitious for that country's level of development. These two factors together mean he was certainly going to be right more often than not. But that does not make it an inevitable economic rule. Differentiating products in the way discussed can suggest to a country where it can play its competition-friendly protectionism cards to achieve progressive goals, and on the other hand where it should defer to the safe and tidy, chaos-sorting predictability of efficient free market forces. It can also suggest where the covert or overt industrial policy rivalry of rich and developing countries needs to be carefully observed and debated, and on the other hand, the industries where it will never be an issue.

The conclusions drawn from this chapter are that three forms of policy can be considered desirable to temper and improve the present free market globalisation path we are on. Diagram B on the back pages of the book illustrates both these three proposed policies and the positive outcomes discussed below. Firstly, rich countries need to choose to protect certain mass-market labour intensive economic activities in order to cause a 'general tightening' at the lower end of their labour markets. Secondly, the very poor countries that are in for a long wait before they can hope to be internationally competitive in manufacturing exports must also choose high-volume labour intensive basic manufacturing to protect. This is not intended to start an export boom, but merely introduce some basic positive externalities and capabilities into these countries. As is also the case regarding rich countries, the priority must be that the products chosen must have large enough markets to engender competition, and not, as in the past, be chosen for their prestige or ambitious technological characteristics. Thirdly, international assistance should be provided to help small, poor countries join together to form regional free trade zones. This will provide them with the intermediate-sized market scope often required to make certain instances of protectionism become viable and competition-friendly.

When the three policies noted above are applied, they combine quite favourably when considered alongside the three biggest problems of our time. These three problems are the depletion and deterioration of our environment, the hopeless poverty of some very poor countries, and growing inequality in many other countries. It may seem that inequality in rich countries is the least significant of the three issues, but as noted in other sections, this particular problem has to be addressed before the rich and powerful countries can move their political and economic attentions onto the other two more fundamental issues. For example, since the current economic downturn, I am sure I have heard less news items regarding climate change and Third World poverty compared with the better times before. The high unemployment and the growth deemed necessary in the present system to cure it have an immediacy that overshadows the other two issues and pushes them onto the back burner. Also, an important role of the rich countries has always been to present an example for other countries to follow, therefore presenting a model of a sustainable stable wealthy economy thriving without perpetual growth, is a very positive contribution. To present more clearly the points made, the following subsections are four pillars of support for the conclusions arrived at.

a) Environmental Constraints and Costs

The issues surrounding the basic conflict between our present rapacious, input-hungry model of capitalist growth and the limited resources and tolerances of our global environment can trump all other issues in the long term. Critics of a protectionist approach will with some justification note that protectionism could reduce the potential of developing countries to benefit from trade. But surely developing countries are at greater fundamental risk of being squeezed out of having access to the earth's limited resources, and therefore it is wrongheaded to prioritise the excessive consumption of rich countries in their name. The demand generated within and between developing countries has now reached a critical mass that can maintain its own growth in trade, without the need to rely on perpetual growth in rich country consumption. If a new approach to international trade can move the economic world in a direction of more limited environmental depletion and damage, or a more environmentally efficient route to relieving extreme poverty, this must be a strong pillar of support for such concepts. In already wealthy countries, stable prosperity without perpetual economic growth should be considered the holy grail of economics.

b) Inequality in Rich and Developing Countries

A theme discussed a few times is the way in which our ever-hungry capitalist system actually forces us to strive towards ever-greater consumption, justified by the need to help the poorest sections of rich countries' societies. The shark has to keep on swimming, and the rich man has to keep getting richer, just to make life OK at the bottom of the heap. An approach to trade that can square this circle of lower environmental consumption and depletion, while not diminishing the opportunities of the poor in rich countries, must have some merit. In the present system, however rich rich countries get, as long as they continually suffer from high unemployment and inequality, growth and therefore further excessive environmental depletion will always be the answer. Unemployment and 'creating jobs' is often the motive for rich countries' selfish actions on the world stage. The best way to reduce these abuses of power performed by the rich countries, like for example some of the widely cited WTO issues, is take away the economic and political pressures motivating its actors. Cracking this unemployment nut would allow greater altruism from them in the future. As shown in diagram B, the policies of selective relocalisation or competition-friendly protectionism could not only *cause* stagnation in GDP growth in rich countries, but also *allow* this to be less painful for the poor, by tightening the lower end of the labour markets. The concepts of competition-friendly protectionism become both the cause and the immunisation in regard to lower GDP growth.

The attribute of reducing inequality, even if this comes at the expense of total wealth, will become more and more attractive to rich countries over time. Problems resulting from unemployment and inequality will become more pronounced within societies, and concerns over wealth loss will seem more and more crude and inappropriate for very rich people in an environmentally deteriorating world. Some avenues of spending extra new income do not generate extra carbon emissions or consume extra environmental resources, but not very many. The fact is that very rich people are bad for the environment. This potential for tackling unemployment and inequality in rich countries is another pillar of support for these concepts.

c) The Equilibrium Principle

The phrase equilibrium principle here refers to a way of thinking that forces countries and policy makers to consider the whole, and not just their part, when considering trade issues. Many dimensions and assumptions of national trade policies and attitudes look selfish, naive or even short-sighted when stepping back and considering them from a global perspective. For a rational analysis of global trade, the starting point must be to recognise that the sum of the parts can only be as large as the whole, and the whole can only be as large as the sum of its parts. World trade opportunities and world demand in each and every market and industry are finite, and therefore policy goals and projections for each and every country must make sense within this fundamental constraint. For a specific illustrative example, as mentioned earlier, many rich and developing countries are planning to be world leaders in new green technology. But the equilibrium principle by pure logic would tell us that all those countries cannot be *leaders* in *all* parts of this industry. To have leaders, you need followers; to have winners, you need losers; to have exporters, you need importers. For rich countries, trade policy in a world of more and more developing countries containing skilled and capitalised workers requires a new way of thinking that takes more account of the rest of the world, and does not rely on the rest of the world accommodating their own country's relative dominance.

A good starting point for any area of life is: Do as you would be done by, or the familiar Bible version, Do unto others as you would have done unto yourself. Likewise, the starting point for true steps towards world equality must be to recognise that individual trade and production outcomes should be made up of countries that more equally reflect and acknowledge the whole. For example, if an investigation into world economic output found there to be a specific mix in the goods globally demanded, produced and consumed, in a truly equal world, that *mix* should be replicated down to country level. For a crude example, imagine the economic world as being divided equally between three levels of positive externality-producing activities: low (commodities, most agriculture), medium (basic manufacturing of simple mature products and average service provision) and high (cutting-edge manufacturing, technology and innovation-led new products and services). Given this knowledge of the whole, and the key value given to positive externalities, the most fundamental basis for equality between countries would be for each country within the whole to contain production of the same breakdown or mix of these gradient groupings. This is the extreme which is not advocated here, but it does illustrate the fundamental inequalities of the present system once an economic activities matter stance is taken. The conclusions of this chapter would seek to reverse to a degree the global division of labour which free market globalisation has encouraged and achieved so dramatically.

The reality of the present is that there is serious pressure on rich countries to remain 'competitive' in order to maintain growth and low unemployment. This forces them to attempt to inhabit as much of the high positive externality economic activities as possible, which motivates a greater international division of labour. This fuels the schizophrenic mode of rich country international relations posture, where they outwardly state that they want both world poverty reduction and to be a country achieving and cornering more than their share of the world's most lucrative and positive externality-rich products. Think for a moment about the incongruity of these two simultaneous aims and stances. A crude analogy would be that it is like grandly stating to the dependent young children of your family that you do not want them to be malnourished, but to grow strong and healthy ... and then with the next breath stating that you are going to eat all the food that comes into the house, except the large bag of rice in the cupboard under the sink, which they are to live on. In this food-themed analogy, sophisticated manufacturing produces the vitamins and minerals required for development, whereas the commodity and agricultural sectors are the bulky but nutritionally limited rice.

This typical international relations stance of rich and powerful countries is schizophrenic because the trade stances and aid stances provide two different and conflicting narratives coming from the same source. Rich countries are *forced* into this stance by the need to survive within this present free trade comparative advantage-based system. Governments of rich and developing countries operating within the present status quo are offered a stark choice: gain a larger share of the best, most positive externality-generating markets by dominating poor countries, or face high unemployment at home. In contrast, this new approach to trade hopes to offer a step towards an alternative resolution of this problem.

Relocalising certain labour-intensive low positive externality goods back into rich countries is a step towards making their economic make-up more accurately reflect the composition of the world economy. The population of rich countries will be producing and providing a more balanced spread of economic activities, which better reflects what they are consuming. This is a small step towards reducing and reversing the international division of labour. The basis of true equality means that the parts more truly reflect the whole, and following these policies would bring this reality a tiny bit closer. It is not suggested here that protectionist policies should be attempting to bridge the positive externality gap between countries overnight, for example by producing cars in Rwanda or sat navs in Niger. The point is that there is some product or service that *could* be of the right modest step up in positive externality, and with the right kind of required scope, which could thrive if protected in these countries. Certain products may be low enough in required scope to thrive when protected in a single country; others may require a revamped regional free trade grouping. But the products and services do exist. The key is to differentiate the right products to fit the market scope required. The equilibrium principle highlights the fallacies of our contemporary economic narratives, and supports the more holistic alternative put forward here.

d) Positive Externalities Matter More than GDP

The silver bullet that supposes to protect the concepts of competition-friendly protectionism from the onslaught of mainstream economic arguments is the claim that positive externalities matter more than GDP regarding development outcomes. Mainstream economic theory can be used effectively to crush most protectionist ideas, through the watertight application of comparative advantage and trade theories. These theories can prove clearly that protectionism destroys GDP wealth. The analysis here does not dispute these mathematically sound trade equations, but disputes whether GDP should be regarded instead as a secondary indicator, as compared to positive externality capability and development. As mentioned earlier, even rich countries are conditioned to crave economic growth, even though on reflection they are more than adequately rich as a whole already. We are like

Pavlov's dog – the ringing bell of GDP growth makes us salivate because we have been conditioned to understand that it is not the growth itself which is so important, but the lower unemployment, lower relative poverty, and economic stability that it engenders. The concept of competition-friendly protectionism could tackle the ills of inequality and unemployment without the need for perpetual GDP growth. This would leave us free to understand and manage the true source of value being generated by economic activity, which is not only monetary gain in the short term, but positive externalities in the long term.

It is possible for a country to be increasing its technology and innovation capabilities and not growing in terms of GDP at the same time. Consider Britain during WWII. It suffered massive economic destruction and had to redeploy its resources away from consumption and towards the massive production of weapons etc that the war effort required. But although a significant proportion of the wealth of the country was lost, the technology and innovation advancements were great. As discussed in chapter seven, although rich countries may lose their ability to continually earn a living off of brand new technology and innovation, this does not mean their consumers cannot continue to enjoy the fruits of these developments, and live higher standards of living even with less trade domination and less relative wealth advantages.

In line with the equilibrium principle outlined above, no country could or should attempt to corner more than its fair share of high positive externality-generating economic activities, but equally, all countries should still aim to have their own talent or prize sector. In Britain, for example, although we bemoan the fact that we have lost much of our manufacturing base and 'don't make anything anymore', we have gems tucked away that are world leaders – for example the Rolls Royce company, which itself no longer makes the cars, but does manufacture a large proportion of the jet engines used for the world's jumbo jet aeroplanes. No country should attempt to do *only* things like this, but every rich and developing country should fight to maintain its *fair share*. Of course, Britain is not as dominant as it once was in industrial manufactured goods, but it has to be understood that Britain's past position of dominance was a highly atypical situation, which could never be reproduced in a world with an ever-growing number of rival advanced countries. This fair share concept is what has been suggested above as a role for a reformed WTO, whereby it is remitted to watch over the horse-trading and negotiation between vying states trying to protect and subsidise their star performers. Name the game of industrial policy for all to recognise, gauge and compare, and then, through organisations like the WTO, share out the spoils.

This primary consideration of valuing positive externalities over GDP growth also must be applied to poor countries. This would imply, as discussed earlier, that it is not necessarily conducive to development for poor and developing countries to be churning out low positive externality products. It is not necessarily harmful for them to be doing this either, as every case requires investigation, but GDP generated by nominally growing economic activity alone is an empty, perishable and reversible activity if it does not engender solid, irreversible steps of positive externality growth. To help poor countries, firstly this approach to trade can reduce the imperative for rich countries to corner all the positive externality-generating economic activities. Secondly, through competition-friendly protectionism within very poor countries, it is possible to provide a modest positive externality stimulus to their economies by selecting certain goods and services with robust markets for them to produce and provide for themselves. In summary, the recognition that positive externalities in the long term can trump pure GDP growth in the short term can defend the concept of competition-friendly protectionism against the genuine argument that wealth losses would result from market interference. The loss of GDP wealth if such policies were followed is not denied; it is just claimed that it is, and will become, of lesser importance than other objectives. This realisation must be a pillar of support for a new approach to international trade.

Diagram B and the four sections above demonstrate what can be argued to be a symmetry of outcomes that become possible when the proposed policies are applied. The proposals here are not a reactionary or anarchistic leap away from the present fundamentally capitalist free market system, but an *accommodation*, like the welfare state. It is evolution, not revolution. It is an evolution because it seeks to analyse and differentiate beyond the black and white ideological generalisations made by both the free trade fundamentalists on one side, and the anti-globalisation reactionaries on the other side. The best answer to ideologically applied generalisation is to differentiate, and this approach to trade and economics seeks to differentiate in many different ways. It seeks to differentiate in a more sophisticated way the different strands that make up the complex web of modern international trade. We do not trade in monotone, formula-friendly widgets, but vastly different products and markets. It seeks to differentiate between purely monetary GDP growth and positive externality growth, which represents not a country's income but its capability. It seeks to differentiate between the maximum scope required by different traded products and *enough* free trade scope. It also seeks to differentiate between *maximum* competition and *enough* competition required to enjoy the well-identified benefits that capitalist competition produces.

It is proposed that this approach to international trade can provide a useful reconciliation between the genuine efficiency, wealth creating and searching qualities of free trade in some circumstances, and the growing recognition that a wholesale free trade world is an unequal and divisive place. Free trade has many qualities as an ideology that should not be ignored, but its outcomes have side effects like concentration and crystallised inequality. The free trade ideology is for now still clinging on as a flag of convenience used by most countries, in an economic theory landscape containing few obvious alternatives. But its weaknesses are becoming more apparent and dissension from the tenets of its ideology by many countries is becoming harder to ignore. Free trade ideals *are* going to be compromised due to political and economic expediency during the next few decades. The proposal here is that it would be preferable to at least have an approach or plan that could pre-empt and accommodate this shift, rather than a continuation of the present policy vacuum, which has led to schizophrenic hypocrisy in international trade relations and discussions.

Practical Issues to Consider

Dealing in theories is fine, but the real world rarely allows the easy conformity of economic reality to economic theory. Below are two practical points relevant to the conclusions made above. Other issues and objections are sure to be found if a competition-friendly protectionism approach were ever to gain support, but these two sections are a starting point at this early stage.

a) Immigration, Europe and Trade Agreements

It can seem lazy and insightful to make immigration an issue, but the fact is that central to the approach of this book is the concept of tightening bottom-end labour markets in rich countries, and this cannot happen if people from poorer countries are entering this same labour market in large numbers.

Detractors may argue that reducing immigration will reduce the opportunities for the migrants and reduce valuable remittances flowing back into poor countries. This may well be true, but the larger issue is deemed to be that rich countries should achieve a stable model of economic existence that can survive without perpetual economic growth. Providing this example to the world and not requiring a perpetually growing portion of the earth's finite resources, in the larger picture, will do more to help poorer countries than helping the minority of determined migrants to improve their own circumstances. Obviously, this is not a racial or anti-foreigner issue, but purely practical.

In Britain's case, for the above policies to work, it would have to leave the European Union in order to stop intra-European immigration. The other option is to treat the EU as the unit for protectionism and labour market tightening. But in current times, the EU seems unlikely to reach the political unity required for such a policy. In this scenario, protectionist policies on the EU as a whole would for the first generation only bring the poorer countries in line with the rest, while the richer countries of the EU would feel no benefit until the time when this levelling had been reached. This is because as things stand at present, there are still different standards of wages in different member countries, and new demand generated by shutting out imports would logically locate in the lower-cost countries within the union. Meanwhile, countries like Britain would be experiencing the higher prices for consumers, but not gaining any new jobs.

Changing Britain's international relations posture away from a nominally free trade façade to openly perusing protectionism as a main policy plank of government would cause major disruptions to international relations and treaty agreements. But the fact is that if unemployment and inequality continue to get worse in rich countries, everything becomes liable for renegotiation by sheer force of political pressure. As the challenges produced by the recent financial crisis have shown, when governments *have to act*, like pumping billions of dollars of support into economies totally against their free market instincts, anything not impossible is possible.

b) Choosing Industries to Protect

In terms of choosing an industry to protect in a rich country, the household furniture industry could be a good example. This is only an illustrative suggestion, as really it is too early in the development of these ideas to be thinking about this end game. It is a large industry that is labour intensive, and it would have quite a clean effect on the country's economy. By "clean", it is meant that the effect of protecting the household furniture industry from imports would indeed push up the price of furniture for consumers in this country, but the effects would be isolated to just this industry. The high price of domestically produced furniture would not affect the competitiveness of other industries' exports. The protected industry would require many workers and therefore contribute in a small way to tightening the bottom end of the national labour market. Furniture would become far more expensive, which would reduce the disposable incomes of every family in the country. Importing no furniture would reduce our total imports by a small fraction, and diverting resources and skewing internal markets would reduce exports by a similar amount. The country would be less well off due to importing less labour intensive goods and exporting less high tech goods, ie, moving away from its comparative advantage. But it would be a step towards having less inequality and unemployment. It could be argued that this is a worthwhile trade-off for a very rich country in an environmentally finite world.

"An invasion of armies can be resisted, but not an idea whose time has come." – Victor Hugo.

Bibliography

Ball, Phillip, *Critical Mass: How One Thing Leads to Another*, Arrow Books, 2005.

Beinhocker, Eric D, *The Origin of Wealth*, Random House, 2006.

Cameron, Rondo, *A Concise Economic History of the World*, Third Edition, Oxford University Press, 1997.

Chang, Ha-Joon, *Bad Samaritans*, Random House, 2007.

Collier, Paul, *The Bottom Billion*, Oxford University Press, 2008.

Cohen, Stephen S., & DeLong, J. Bradford, *The End of Influence*, Basic Books, 2010.

Das, Bhagirath lal, *The World Trade Organisation*, Zed Books, 1999.

De Rivero, Oswaldo, *The Myth Of Development*, Zed Books, 2001.

Dumas, Charles & Choyleva, Diana, *The Bill from the China Shop*, Profile Books, 2006.

Easterly, William, *The White Man's Burden*, Oxford University Press, 2006.

Friedman, Thomas, *The Lexus and The Olive Tree*, Harper Collins, 2000.

Henderson, J. Vernon, Shalizi, Zmarak & Venables, Anthony J. *Geography and Development*," World Bank Internet Resource, 1999

Jawara, Fatoumata & Kwa, Aileen, *Behind the Scenes at the WTO*, Zed Books, 2003.

Krugman, Paul R., *Rethinking International Trade*, MIT Press, 2000.

Perkins, John, *Confessions of an Economic Hit Man*, Ebury Press, 2005.

Prestowitz, Clyde, *Three Billion New Capitalists*, Basic Books, 2005.

Reich, Robert, *Supercapitalism*, Icon Books, 2008.

Reinert, Erik S, *How Rich Countries Got Rich, And Why Poor Countries Stay Poor*, Constable, 2007.

Woodman, Conor, *Unfair Trade*, Random House Business Books, 2011.

DIAGRAM A:

DIFFERENTIATION IN TRADED MANUFACTURED GOODS

LARGE MARKET SIZE REQUIRED FOR VIABILITY	**L A R G E**	LOW FIXED COSTS AND / OR LOW ECONOMIES OF SCALE *BUT STILL REQUIRES LARGE SCOPE AS VERY SPARSELY DEMANDED*
SPARSE & OR SPECIALIST DEMAND	**>**	HIGH FIXED COSTS AND / OR HIGH ECONOMIES OF SCALE *LARGE SCOPE REQUIRED AS EXPECTED*
SCOPE REQUIRED ∧ ∨		
SMALL MARKET SIZE REQUIRED FOR VIABILITY	**>**	HIGH FIXED COSTS AND / OR HIGH ECONOMIES OF SCALE *BUT ONLY REQUIRES LITTLE SCOPE AS VERY HEAVILY DEMANDED*
DENSE & OR MASS- MARKET DEMAND	**S M A L L**	LOW FIXED COSTS AND / OR LOW ECONOMIES OF SCALE *LITTLE SCOPE REQUIRED AS EXPECTED*

*(POSITIVE EXTERNALITIES OTHER THAN ECONOMIES)
(OF SCALE WHICH IS REPRESENTED ON THE OTHER AXIS)

FREE TRADE SECTOR	
(EG A WOVEN LAUNDRY BASKET)	(EG A PAIR OF SKIING GOGGLES)
~CHECK INDUSTRIAL POLICY TO A MINIMUM	
~MAXIMUM FREE MARKET COMPETITION, TECHNOLOGY & INNOVATION OF GLOBAL BEST REQUIRED	
"THE INVISABLE HAND & FREE MARKET RULES & THEORIES SHOULD APPLY"	

EMULATION SECTOR	**PRIZE SECTOR**
(EG A PLASTIC GARDEN RAKE)	(EG MUSIC RECORDING EQUIPMENT)
~LEAVE AS NOW TO EXPORT LED GROWTH	
~LEADING DEVELOPING COUNTRIES SERVING GLOBAL MARKETS	~REQUIRES RECOGNITION OF INDUSTRIAL POLICY AS BEING HIGHLY POTENT HERE
	~NAME THE GAME, FLAG UP THE BIG PLAYERS.
"THE LUCKY FEW DEVELOP"	~EXCESSIVE INDUSTRIAL POLICY OF LEAD
RELOCALISATION SECTOR	COUNTRIES THEREFORE TO BE SCRUTINISED
(EG A CHEST OF DRAWERS)	& BARTERED PERHAPS THROUGH WTO
~PROTECTION VIABLE IF MARKET LARGE ENOUGH TO ENGENDER NEAR OPTIMUM COMPETITION	*"ECONOMIC ACTIVITIES MATTER, THEREFORE BUSINESS IS WAR"*
	(EG A CAR ENGINE OR A SILICONE CHIP)
~DEFER TO PROGRESSIVE GOALS	**SMALL BUSINESS SECTOR**
HIGH FIXED COST IN RICH COUNTRIES	(EG A CARAVAN)
LOW FIXED COSTS IN POOR COUNTRIES	~BUSINESSES NOT LIKELY TO GROW LARGE
	~R&D SUBSIDY MORE SIGNIFICANT THAN
"THE LEAST WORST WAY TO BUY EQUALITY"	PROTECTIONISM WHEN COMPARING THE INDUSTRIAL POLICY OF STATES
(EG A BASIC WOODEN TABLE & CHAIRS)	*"SOURCE OF VIBRANT SM"L BUS" ECOLOGY"*
LOW ^	^ **HIGH**

POSITIVE EXTERNALITIES* TO BE HAD FROM PROVISION

< MATURE & UNDYNAMIC	EVOLVING & PIONEERING >
< COMMODIFIED & STEADY	PROFITABLE & HIT OR MISS >

DIAGRAM B:
THE SYMMETRY OF OUTCOMES

POLICY (i)

RELOCALISATION OF SPECIFIC LABOUR INTENSIVE SECTORS BACK TO RICH COUNTRIES.

>>> **EFFECT (i)**

MORE RELATIVE DEMAND FOR LOWER END OF LABOUR MARKET IN RICH COUNTRIES. "TIGHTENING" OF LABOUR MARKET.

POLICY (ii)

LOCALISATION OF SPECIFIC SECTORS WITH ROBUST MARKETS AND SUITABLE REQUIRED SCOPE INTO POOR COUNTRIES.

>> **EFFECT (ii)**

LOSS OF THE WELL PROVEN WEALTH EFFECTS OF TRADE. (COMPARATIVE ADVANTAGE)

POLICY (iii)

REATTEMPTING REGIONAL TRADE AGREEMENTS BETWEEN POOR COUNTRIES.

>>> **EFFECT (iii)**

GREATER AMOUNT OF POSITIVE EXTERNALITY RICH PRODUCTS MADE IN POOR COUNTRIES.

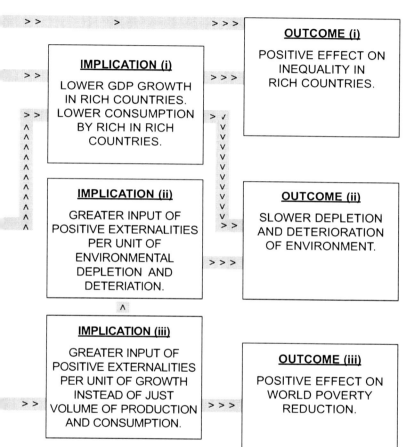

Lightning Source UK Ltd.
Milton Keynes UK
UKOW04f2126290116

267417UK00001B/11/P